Quote

'... before the changes of Vatic؛ ____amil-
iar to all of us who lived it, but ____.n as Mars to the
uninitiated.' Sister Pauline Engel, ؟ ____ʋʀʂ

'...though ... she writes with a humorous acceptance and surprising gratitude for the experience within the priory, she is quite clear about the horror of a system that, for her, denied individuality and stifled creativity. Marion McLeod, *The New Zealand Listener*

'It so touched people's hearts the mail hasn't stopped coming in.' Leigh Bramwell, *Next*

'... a special insight into a rare sort of person. Her story demanded that I read it in one sitting. I am not surprised the book sold out within 10 days of publication.' Kay Williams, *Evening Standard*

'The story is riveting. But it is the writing that delivers the story, after all.' Jane Tolerton, *The Waikato Times*

'A very warm and human tale, telling how a free spirit overcame a system designed to supress individualism.' *Ashburton Guardian*

'This could almost be one of those "all you ever wanted to know about but could not find out no matter how hard you tried" books.' Chris James, *Otago Daily Times*

'This is an uplifting book.' *Christchurch Star*

# Breaking the Habit

## Life in a New Zealand Convent
## 1955–67

## Judith Graham

Longacre Press

ISBN 1 877361 44 5

First published by John McIndoe Ltd, 1992
Reprinted 1992, 1996

This edition published by Longacre Press, 2006
30 Moray Place, Dunedin, New Zealand.

A catalogue record for this book is available
from the National Library of New Zealand.

Cover and book design by Christine Buess.
Printed by Astra Print, New Zealand.

# CONTENTS

# PREFACE

ONE afternoon, visiting my eighty-six year old mother, I found a photograph of me as a nun. 'Who's this?' I asked. 'A girl I once knew,' she replied. I flinched, but remembering the remark years later, I thought it could have been a great title for this book. When the book was first published in 1992, I was surprised at how well it was received because I had intended it to be an historical account for my children and for theirs of my early life. I knew then that that way of life was disappearing fast in a changing world, but it appealed to a much wider audience. Was that because it satisfied a curiosity about nuns? Or was it because it was a personal story about someone's journey towards self-knowledge? A journey we all take, though mine was somewhat off the main route. Whatever the reason, here again is the story of a girl I once knew and with whom I can still live.

*Judith Graham, 2006*

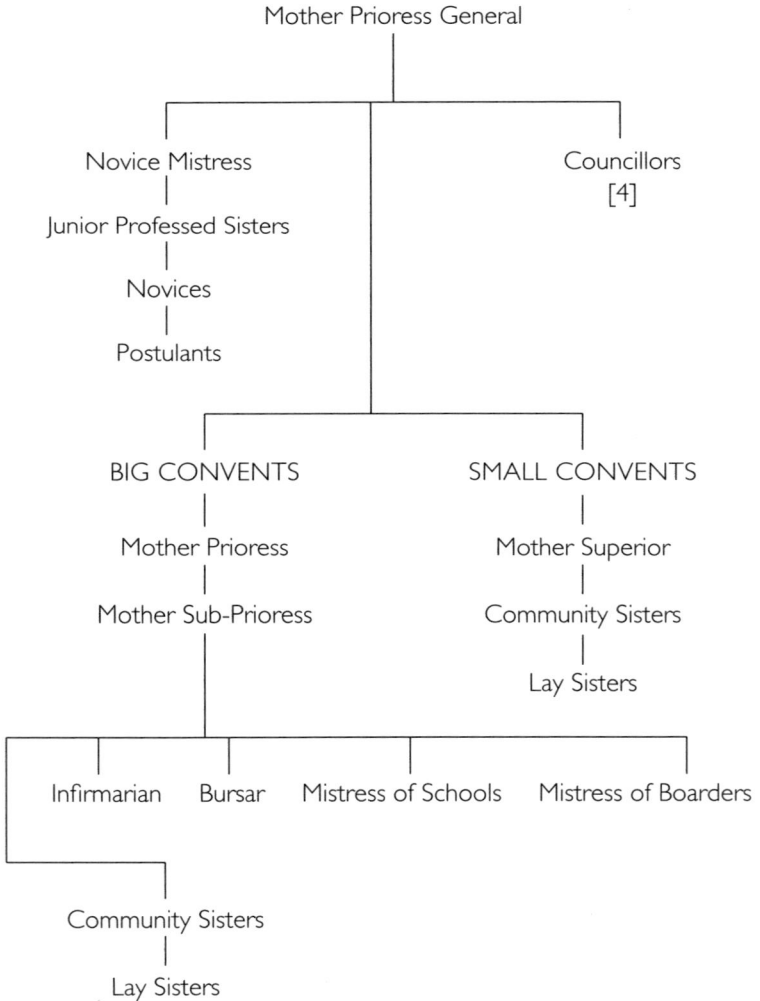

# MOTHER HOUSE

Mother Prioress General

Novice Mistress

Junior Professed Sisters

Novices

Postulants

Councillors
[4]

BIG CONVENTS

Mother Prioress

Mother Sub-Prioress

Infirmarian    Bursar    Mistress of Schools    Mistress of Boarders

Community Sisters

Lay Sisters

SMALL CONVENTS

Mother Superior

Community Sisters

Lay Sisters

# FOREWORD

When I was small, which is many years and kilograms ago, my father promised me half a crown if I could keep a diary faithfully for a year. He thought it would encourage me in the discipline of writing. Twenty years later he told me to write this book. And now, another twenty-five years on, facing retirement and a memory that is quickly fading, I recall my life as I see it.

For him – and for my mother – in gratitude.

And for Reg, Kirsty and Piers, by way of explanation...

*Judith Graham, 1992*

# CHAPTER 1

# PAPANUI CHILDHOOD

WHEN I was seven years old my mother, like all other Catholic mothers, dressed me as a miniature bride. This was for the most important event of my Catholic childhood. I was to make my first Holy Communion with all the others in standard one at St Joseph's School, Papanui. We were to receive the Body of Christ in the form of an altar bread for the first time. Even my sandals and socks were white and on either side of the veil I wore on my head were two bunches of lily of the valley. Their smell, and the music of the First Communion hymn, 'O Mary Mother, sweetest, best', are my strongest sensual memories of childhood.

The day before Holy Communion we all made our first confessions. Father Timoney was our parish priest, a kindly Irishman who was to hear our confessions after Sister had trained us in the various kinds of sin we could have committed – disobedience, lying, unkindness. We learnt about mortal and venial sins: mortal sins meant hell if we died before we had confessed them. To commit a mortal sin required three things: full knowledge, serious matter, and full consent to the evil. If one of these conditions was missing, the sin was venial. All this was laid out in the catechism which we learnt by heart every day. Life was full of terrifying certainties and the most certain of all was death.

If we died not in the state of grace we would go to hell for ever and ever. At the age of seven I found the whole idea of eternity terrifying. And an eternity of hell was unthinkable. Most of the fairy stories I heard ended with the words 'and they lived happily ever after', but there wasn't much about happiness in the catechism. If you made it to Heaven you were a dead cert for happiness but 'God made me to know Him, love Him and serve Him in this world and to be happy for ever with Him in the next'. It seemed a long wait for happiness.

At St Joseph's we were taught in the old chapel school and we were seated in twos at cramped desks on the uneven, rutted floor. The blackboard in front of us had a beautiful border of flowers and grapes wrought in coloured chalks. At the top under the crucifix were the initials AMDG – *ad maiorem gloriam Dei*. We had no idea in standard four what that meant but it was something to do with getting our tables right. We stood in line in front of the board where Sister Aloysius had drawn a clock without hands. When she pointed to two figures we had to add or subtract immediately or move to the bottom of the line, getting a whack over the palm of our hands for not 'knowing our mental'. The sevens table was my frequent undoing.

I was beginning to become a hated goody-goody by about standard four. To be a saint like the popular St Therese of

Lisieux, or 'Little Flower' as she was called, was something we were all taught to aspire to – I took it very seriously. Being a saint meant praying a lot, making Acts – eating what we hated, smiling at people who laughed at us or said things like 'You're a fatty'. It especially meant we had to be different from those around us. My mother told me to look at the fir tree – 'The nearer you are to God, the lonelier you are. There aren't many branches at the top.'

Being a saint also meant I had to please God in all I did.

I decided the best way to begin any day was to get up at 6.30am and bike to mass at St Joseph's, our parish church, about fifteen minutes away. There weren't many people there and I felt special going into the semi-lit church, smelling the candles and kneeling in the shadows with the seven or eight adults.

One morning Father Timoney said before he started mass, 'I've no altar server. Would you act as altar boy, please Judith?' I was terrified. Girls were not allowed in the sanctuary unless they were cleaning it or setting the altar or arranging the flowers. I hadn't ever read the Latin aloud but I couldn't refuse either. I went up to the altar rails and knelt down with my missal open. '*Introibo ad altare Dei*,' he began. '*Ad Deum qui lae...ti...fi...cat iu..ven...tu...tem meam*'. I stumbled over each syllable and it was a great relief when the *Introit* of the mass was over and Father had it on his own. But it all added to the exclusive feeling of going to daily mass early in the morning. It took about forty minutes, then I went back home for breakfast and off again on the same route, this time to school.

My best primary school friend was Catherine Dowling.

She lived with her sister, two older brothers and a widowed mother on a farm near the Styx river in Belfast on the outskirts of Christchurch. I was often allowed to bike home with her after school to play for an hour of marvellous freedom in the wide open paddocks by the river instead of in our neat and boxed in backyard. Catherine was a wonderfully loyal friend but I was to lose all contact with her when my parents decided my sister and I needed some social polishing and sent us off on our bikes to standard five and six at St Mary's College in Colombo Street.

St Mary's was a considerable step up from the parish school. For one thing, there were no boys and there were only about ten of us in standard five. I realised that I lived in a state house and most of the class lived in what seemed to me to be palaces in Fendalton. Then too, Sister Lelia had taught me at St Joseph's and welcomed me with open arms at St Mary's, making me a class prefect. I had a miserable year as the teacher's pet.

# CHAPTER 2

# GENETIC CONNECTIONS

BEING the eldest in a wartime household was a responsible business. My father had left for Italy about five months after his first and only son was born. At night in our little house in Union Street, Papanui, the blinds were pulled down and kept down by heavy books to stop any chinks of light which might give away our whereabouts to enemy planes. There was a special urgency when the air raid sirens went. I knew about the Japanese. There were frightening comics we got from school friends which showed people having their fingernails pulled off by evil-looking Japanese soldiers.

Before the war my father was a young journalist on the *Christchurch Press*. My most abiding memory of him is his typing at his desk in the front bedroom. He was twenty-five when I was born, and was small in height and build. He had been educated at St Bede's right through to matriculation and that was quite noteworthy in those days. Only the intervention of one kindly Marist Father had stopped his leaving school earlier and he was forever grateful.

The *Press* was a paper widely respected and my father loved it and all it stood for. All his life his closest friends were journalists though I'm sure he found it difficult to be accepted at first. Being a Catholic, he was an outsider in that establishment. That may sound strange now but in the 1930s Christchurch expected its prominent and respectable citizens to be both Anglican and of English descent.

My father met my mother in Christchurch in 1935. She had felt disgraced in Dunedin after her parents' divorce and left to work as a nursing sister in psychiatric hospitals in the North Island. She wanted to be a nun and joined The Home of Compassion, founded by Mother Aubert, whom she passionately admired. However she was not permitted to take vows in that Order partly because her parents had divorced and this might cause a scandal. In great sadness she left and was later recruited by another religious Order of missionary Sisters working in the Pacific Islands. She was accepted by them for training in America but found the Order very different in approach from The Home of Compassion and very provincial French in its outlook. Taking a bath in a chemise did not fit in with a New Zealander's perception of either sanctity or hygiene.

She left the Order and returned to Christchurch where she was introduced to my father by a mutual friend. She was three years older than he and seven inches taller. But she was strikingly beautiful with black hair and strong blue eyes, and often compared with Joan Crawford. My father was smitten, countering all her rebuffs with passionate letters and they were eventually married in October 1936 at St Joseph's Cathedral, Dunedin. My mother was always conscious of the height difference and even their wedding photo is taken from the waist up as she was standing on a lower step.

The tiny state house at 17 Union Street was our first family home. It was two-bedroomed and Gillian and Emmet, who arrived at respectable two-yearly intervals shared the back bedroom with me. When it was wet, this was where we played endless games of keeping house for a large family of dolls, Gillian and Emmet as helpers and me as a very bossy mother. It was much greater fun playing outside on warm nor'west nights. Flushed with excitement we came unwillingly inside when the bath was ready and were very efficiently processed through the cleaning ritual by our mother. In bed, smelling of Cashmere Bouquet, we listened enchanted as she read us *Little Women* or *Lassie* or *Anne of Green Gables* before kissing us goodnight. 'Goodnight, Mummy. God bless you.'

She was very much a solo mother because until my father went away with the Second NZEF in 1941 he was either away at work at night or asleep during the daylight hours. All our breakfasts were punctuated by my mother repeating, 'Don't wake your father', and we would tiptoe and whisper round the house until we could whoop off to school with great shouts of relief.

Our mother was, therefore, the disciplinarian. She also lit fires, chopped wood, mowed lawns, prepared an entire section for the vegetable and flower gardens, put out rubbish, paid the bills, organised the budget. My father was blissfully irresponsible over such things and this was the cause of very real argument and frustration for my mother. But to us as children he was a boon companion and a storyteller beyond compare.

We missed him greatly during the war, but his home-coming was a surprisingly tense time. My mother hated making an exhibition of any affection. She refused to go to the station to meet him but waited at home. I was terribly excited but my brother Emmet was hopelessly confused. He had never known this stranger who was coming to live with us. For so many families these post-war marital reunions were fraught with tension and it was no surprise that my father soon accepted a job in the parliamentary press gallery (seen by many as a plum job). He lived by himself in Wellington from 1947 till 1949, giving both himself and our mother space to adjust. But from then on the marriage was a damaged one, torn apart by my father's frequent drinking bouts and my mother's terrible screaming rages.

Some reconciliation must have taken place between my parents for in 1947 our youngest sister, Marian, was born. I was overjoyed. My mother's hospital suitcase had been packed and sitting for weeks in their bedroom and one morning it was gone. Gillian, Emmet and I rushed at our sleeping father – 'What is it? A girl or a boy?' He turned over heavily and grunted, 'a girl'. Emmet burst into tears and ran from the room. He was inconsolable for hours.

Being now six of a family we qualified for a bigger state house and moved in 1948 to 140 Harewood Road, just by the town boundary. It was a luxury to have three bedrooms and a larger living area with such a long back yard. My mother set about making a garden and hedging us in from the rude stare of the outside world. It was a mammoth job to convert a paddock but with her usual efficiency and creativity she soon had a very pleasant treed garden behind high hedges on all sides. I remember hydrangeas and roses, geraniums and wisteria, and leafy areas under fruit trees and chestnuts.

It was to this house then that I came home one day in late 1949 to see an envelope in beautiful handwriting lying on the dining room table. It was addressed to my mother and had been sent from Dunedin. 'How do you feel about boarding school?' my mother said. Midnight feasts, best friends of unswerving loyalty, all the heroines of *Girls' Own* books orbited into my imagination. 'I'd love it,' I said. Mother Patricia, one of my mother's teachers in Dunedin, had asked if she would like to send her daughters to her old school. It meant a stupendous effort to get the necessary money saved for fees and the uniform, but my mother felt that this was the school she wanted for us.

First the shiny brown tin trunk appeared in the bedroom and every night I looked at it before I went to sleep, imagining what it would be like unpacking it in a dormitory. The uniform was black and white with lisle stockings. There was a blazer with the Dominican crest on it. There was also a black velvet dress with a cream satin collar and cuffs trimmed with lace to be worn on Saturdays at High Tea. Everything smelled new and as each item was gradually acquired it was folded and carefully packed into the tin trunk. This tin trunk caused my younger sister Gillian and me much embarrassment when a year later it burst its lock and revealed all on the Dunedin railway station – all especially meaning the rows and rows of pure white sanitary towels which my mother had packed as the icing on the layers of our clothes underneath.

The first of these train journeys to Dunedin was enchanting. I didn't feel at all homesick when the morning came for us to catch the southbound express. Emmet and Gillian treated me with the greatest respect – I was off on the big adventure. My mother came with me and after the flatness of Canterbury I found the coastline from Oamaru with the sea curling up towards the bushy hills captivating. This was the beginning of my love affair with Dunedin – its bracing climate, the beauty of its harbour setting and solidity of its Victorian buildings; it appeared so permanent, so secure. St Dominic's boarding establishment for young ladies was up Rattray Street and it looked enormous from the taxi window. My mother didn't talk much about it except to say, 'the Dominicans are ladies – you must not let me down.'

# CHAPTER 3

# 'THE DOMINICANS ARE LADIES'

THERE were about fifteen new boarders in form three in 1950 and I quickly formed a friendship with Fleur Sloane. She hadn't come from far – her parents lived at Seacliff where her father was manager of the psychiatric hospital. She was warm and friendly and great fun. I found her enormously positive attitude a great help as I stood in that vast building. My mother had left me a few hours before and a senior took me up to the dressing room and the Green Dormitory where all the third formers slept. I was speechless looking up at the stair well, four storeys high, the stairs covered with polished brown lino. The solid walls were painted red up to the top of the dado and were cold and damp to touch even in February. The upper portions of the walls were hung with large portraits of biblical scenes. Half way up the stairs was a statue of a monk dressed in black and white and carrying an arum lily. This was St Dominic. Beside him was a glass display case of brightly coloured stuffed birds, a museum piece that looked as if it had been there for a thousand years.

The other new boarders were unpacking noisily in the dormitory. There was Nola from Gore, Elizabeth from Omakau, Helen from Queenstown, Patricia from Palmerston, Bridget from Oamaru, Therese from Kingston; people from places I'd never heard of. Fleur tried out the beds and found them hard. They had horsehair mattresses on wire springs. Each bed was a narrow four-poster with brass rails from which hung curtains on three sides. This formed a cubicle so that we each had a bed and a wooden chair beside it for our underclothes. The floor was of highly polished wood and the whole room of twenty-five beds was to be 'heated' by a tiny gas heater in the middle. The view over the city and harbour from the long narrow windows was superb but I felt a world away from the city below in this concrete fortress. Therese's older sister who had left St Dominic's the year before helped her unpack. A lot of seniors came in to see her and I was very impressed that she knew so many important people already. But it was Therese who cried with homesickness that night in the bed beside mine. I didn't sleep much as I was too excited.

At 7.15 the next morning a Sister came in and clapped her hands twice. Everyone began moving and I soon realised that the 'clap' was the signal for any activity to commence. We learnt to tell the mood of the Sister by the acoustics of her particular clap. We washed and dressed modestly; I found it very hard trying to fasten my bra with a dressing gown draped round my shoulders. Fleur was much more expert. This took place in the Dressing Room, a long room with two rows of basins stretching down its centre. Here we kept our facecloth, soap, hair brushes, nail brushes and toothpaste. When we had finished using the basin we had to dry it out with a towel, giving the taps a special rub. Round the walls of the Dressing Room were wooden lockers where we kept our clothes neatly folded on numbered shelves and hung our uniforms, dressing gowns and Saturday dresses. Once a week these were inspected for tidiness. After dressing we lined up in twos and marched down the four flights of polished stairs to breakfast, pausing on each landing to wait for the next clap in order to proceed. The hymn before breakfast was 'Soul of my Saviour'. Every movement 'in group' up and down those stairs with their iron balustrade was accompanied by hymn singing, often with quite incongruous words – 'Jesus, the very thought of Thee with sweetness fills my breast' – while I was wondering if there was enough hot water for my bath.

The children's refectory was on the ground floor below street level and we approached it through a wide, dark corridor, past the Boot Room where our polished shoes, our coats and hats were kept in numbered rows. Before the refectory door was a little pantry where the infirmary cupboards held cures in bottles for all our woes. The Infirmarian in 1950 was an elderly Sister unhappily called Sister Felicitas who firmly believed that quinine cured everything from toothache to menstrual pain, and we soon learned to put up with any anguish rather than have to swallow such a medicine.

Meals in the refectory in those post-war years were at first lean affairs. There were about fourteen of us at each of the four main tables which were covered with white linen cloths. Each table had two plates of butter, a square of two ounces which had to be divided into seven pieces – a fatty noughts and crosses division so that each girl could have a fair share. We were always ravenously hungry and cold, having had to remove our cardigans and blazers before entering the refectory which was 'warmed' like most of the rooms by a hopelessly inadequate gas heater. On the wall facing the heater was a magnificent framed tapestry of Mary Queen of Scots arriving somewhere – she always looked warm and well-fed to me. Every morning we had stewed fruit, mostly prunes or figs to keep us 'regular', and Weetbix with hot milk, the skin formed thickly on top. On Sunday mornings we had sausages cooked the night before and reheated in the oven after morning mass. Once Mother Gertrude poured the contents of the cocoa jug over them instead of the gravy and the taste was greatly improved. The main meal was at midday and it was utterly predictable. Cold meat on Monday, cubes of gristly meat swimming in gruel on Tuesday (Stewsday), hard, dry, baked chops on Wednesday, bland mince on Thursday and – what I hated most of all – blobs of steamed fish floating in white sauce on Friday. But returning from mass at the cathedral on Sunday we were greeted by the truly divine smell of roast meat. We looked forward to it from one Sunday to the next. Puddings were nearly always fillers, like spotted dick drowned in custard.

We filed into the refectory in silent pairs, said grace, sat and waited for the clap to begin talking. One lunch hour I whispered to Fleur that she could have my rice pudding which I knew was coming. The signal to speak had not yet been given. Sister Reginald had sharp ears: 'Who was speaking at this table?' I kept my eyes down though I felt myself going red. 'Who was speaking? If the person does not own up there will be silence at lunch for everybody all week.' I pushed my chair back noisily and stood up. 'Very well, Judith. You will stand for the whole of lunch and your table will eat in silence because of your lack of self-control.' It was futile to argue.

We had to eat everything put in front of us and sometimes that proved impossible. So we either waited till Sister passed our table and quickly gave the stodgy macaroni cheese to someone near us who was starving and could eat anything or like Therese, well schooled by her older sisters, we kept empty Chesdale cheese packets in the napkin compartment. We forked the mess on our plate quickly into these packets and removed them later, before they became too smelly, into the rubbish tin. Therese often forgot and the combined smells of deteriorating steamed fish, sago pudding and cauliflower cheese greeted our noses by the end of the week.

One morning at breakfast Mother Gertrude served a fourth former a plate of two cream buns. She had been seen walking up Rattray Street eating the third bun while in uniform and such uncouth behaviour was to be punished. Manners were strictly supervised. If someone had to ask you to pass something on the table, then you were failing in your concern for others.

My favourite room was the Study Hall on the first floor with its high Gothic windows and beautifully carved panelling up to shoulder height (a curse to have to dust), its Honours board and the double desks that my mother had sat in when she was at school. It too had the usual highly polished floor and an elaborate desk on the rostrum where the supervising Sister presided on duty. We moved into the Study Hall at half-past four after an hour of Recreation when school had finished. We stayed there until tea at six, then from six-thirty to seven o'clock we had Recreation when we could lie out on the grass behind the cathedral making daisy chains and gossiping. If it was wet we used the Recreation Room on the ground floor. I hated this room because it looked so drab, the plain walls lined with wooden benches. The fireplace was never used and it was always cold. Down one end was an old piano standing somewhat drunkenly on the polished but uneven wooden floor. Here we learned ballroom dancing, taking turns to lead each other in the Maxina, the Gay Gordons and the Scottische. Pat O'Meara played the piano very well and sometimes slipped in the popular hits for us to foxtrot or waltz to – 'The Tennessee Waltz', or 'How Much is that Doggie in the Window'. We had lots of fun in that room in spite of the cold and drabness and the fact that there was always a Sister on duty to stop us from being too noisy.

From seven till eight-thirty we did another stint of study then began the ritual of going to bed. We hymned our way up to the Dressing Room, undressed and, at a clap, began to brush our hair with a hundred strokes. Another clap, and we cleaned our brushes and took them up to the Sister on duty for inspection, holding them up so that she could scrutinise our fingernails as well. We then washed as much of ourselves as we could under a dressing gown and fell onto the horsehair mattresses for a deep sleep.

Every Saturday evening before tea we had a half hour session of Rules in the Study Hall. These were said to be a practice for the last Day of Judgement when all our actions would be scrutinised publicly by a just God – Fleur thought He would be bored stupid. The Mistress of Boarders in my five years always managed to make this half hour a frightening time, so that I had little appetite for High Tea which followed. This was the meal for which we wore our black velvet dresses and during which we were required to speak only in French. First at Rules, Mother would read from an old manuscript with very fine pages about how to conduct ourselves at table; to lift a cup of tea without obviously curling the little finger and to avoid eating peas with a knife or puncturing them with a fork. Then she passed to weightier topics, like our general behaviour. Class by class, starting with the juniors, miscreants were called out, made to stand upright and silent by their desks and accept *without excuse* a charge of misconduct with its appropriate punishment. The whole exercise was designed to shame the offender and it worked. On one occasion, my name was called out. I stood up and Mother Gertrude asked one of the standard one girls to step forward and tie up her shoe laces. This was to show me the correct way of doing things. I had been observed lifting my foot up onto the Dressing Room handbasin. To this day I still kneel to lace up shoes and I hope God has recorded the improvement.

# Chapter 4

# The Perils of Education

IN my first year at boarding school food became an obsession. Several affluent parents regularly sent their offspring enormous tuck boxes of food and soon a gourmet clique formed. Tuck box recipients held feasts on the bottom green with their friends but Fleur and I had no boxes and we were therefore not invited. We watched from a distance. In 1951 a new Mistress of Boarders, Mother Gertrude, was appointed and she stopped the practice quite dramatically. All tuck boxes were taken to the refectory one afternoon and their contents shared with all the boarders. This caused a great deal of indignant muttering but there were no more tuck boxes.

Mother Gertrude was Mistress of Boarders for most of my boarding years. She was a beautiful looking woman with very fine eyes that she could use to great effect. I don't recall that she ever lost her temper with any of us; nuns didn't. But she could make you feel guilty by just looking. One day she told me to examine my conscience and waited six hours before calling me to her office. 'Well?' she asked. I blurted out every sin I could think of, including curling my hair (vanity and presumption). She looked up from her writing, let her eyes rest on my head and murmured to herself, 'I wouldn't have guessed...'

Our weekends were always busy and minutely regulated so that we had little time for homesickness. On Saturday mornings we were allowed to wear our 'home' clothes while we sponged down and pressed our uniforms for the coming week. It was easier also to tackle the 'house duties' in civvies. We were allocated duties for the year working alongside a Sister to clean the boarding school, parlours, glass music rooms (wiping the piano keys with kerosene) and chapel, where we learnt to polish brass candlesticks and vases *perfectly*. Saturday afternoons we sewed while listening to the requests on 4ZB. I was absolutely hopeless at sewing and still remember the frustration and shame I felt when the sewing teacher held up the shapeless pyjamas I was making for everyone to laugh at. I spent all my sewing classes unpicking every seam I ever put together.

At three o'clock on a Saturday we moved to the refectory for enormous sugar buns and cocoa, changed back into our uniforms and went out hatted and gloved in long lines two by two for walks around select parts of Dunedin. Mother Gertrude with remarkable liberality allowed us to go further and further afield and there are photographs of us in high form at the then Highcliff café, the Ross Creek reservoir and the Signal Hill monument. We were once followed down George Street by two drunken sailors fascinated by the long crocodile of uniformed school girls. They got bored before we did.

Form four was traumatic in one way for me. My mother like so many others of her generation had found it difficult to talk about that great irony called the facts of life. She had given me a plain-wrapped book called *Growing Up* and prayed, she told me later, that I'd understand only as much as I needed to. Her prayer was answered and I was left in cruel ignorance. Next door to our classrooms in Rosary Hall were the wild and marvellous boys who went to Christian Brothers and with whom No Contact was permitted.

I fell madly in love with several delicious lads, most of whom were happily unaware of their good fortune. But Bill was; after a school fair in form four he kissed me – behind the school bike sheds, of course. Two other boarders saw it and that night they bailed me up outside the bathroom. 'You know you're going to have a baby.' I looked astonished. 'Of course you are. Kissing's how it all starts.' For a long, long week I was miserable. I couldn't eat or sleep. Who was there to talk to? It says something about the calibre of the senior boarders that Clare, one of the most approachable, noticed my misery, asked without making me squirm with embarrassment and treated me with kindly seriousness. She told me that babies didn't come as easily as that as I'd find out one day and that I couldn't possibly be pregnant. I didn't want to know any more – only that I wouldn't suddenly balloon out of my uniform. The relief was unbelievable.

On the fourth Sunday of every month the boarders were allowed to visit relatives. There weren't very many boarders who came from Christchurch; I had to rely on friends in the day school to take me out from ten till five o'clock. Then in the fourth form a friend of my mother's with three boys at Christian Brothers (an exciting bonus) invited me out. Maureen had a husky voice and a wonderful sense of humour. She knew the ironies of life. She treated me like a friend rather than a friend's daughter and filled me with chocolate cake and fantastic stories of her own teenage exploits. I looked at my mother with new respect.

Other than fourth Sundays boarders rarely went down the street. Sometimes we were sent out for messages to the elegance of Brown Ewing's or the popular DIC. But a Miss Ritchie who lived in the room next to the children's infirmary was the official messenger for the nuns – she even had a special name, *sole touriere*. When she died we were entrusted with small messages but never further north than Arthur Barnett's, the daylight store. Other excursions outside the convent were for Sports Day, held on a patch of green near the Town Belt, whimsically called Robin Hood. We were strictly forbidden to go anywhere near a den of iniquity called the Beau Monde with its jukeboxes, milkbar cowboys and Dunedin's own version of 'juvenile delinquents'. Some fast day girls in the fifth form enhanced their reputation enormously by graphic accounts of what had happened to them in the Beau Monde.

But we boarders never really felt that we belonged in this Presbyterian city. We were taught that Catholics were a chosen people and we had little contact with those we presumptuously referred to as 'non-Catholics'. Somehow they constituted a threat to our faith. Ours was the One True Faith and it had to be defended. We learnt debating skills and public speaking skills so that we could argue with those who questioned or ridiculed our beliefs. Mixed marriages (between a Catholic and a non-Catholic) were described in the catechism as 'dangerous to our faith'. The Church reinforced this message by not allowing couples in a mixed marriage to have a Nuptial Mass. Earlier, couples even had to pronounce their vows in the sacristy, a robing room at the back of the altar.

As Catholic school girls in a Presbyterian city we lived in a small, exclusive clique. It wasn't so much elitist as a kind of military preparedness for attacks from the enemy. My sister Gill made her first non-Catholic friends at university – and survived.

During Christian Doctrine lessons Mother Saint Joan talked to us about martyrdom. Did we have the courage to die for our faith? 'What would you do?' she asked, 'if Communists burst into this class one morning and asked all those who believed in God to stand up? Would you?' I looked blank. I couldn't imagine myself rushing forward. Fleur whispered that she would open her desk and pretend to be looking for a book.

Most Christian Doctrine lessons dealt with morality – the way Catholics ought to behave in any circumstance. There was a set of definite rules to which we must measure up. Decisions in life were not easy. If a pregnant woman knew she faced probable death in giving birth to her baby she should go ahead and give birth. Her life should be surrendered that the baby might live. I thought that this seemed awfully unfair to her husband and her other children as well as to her, but that was the rule. I hated the law that if you died unbaptised you didn't have a show, ever, of getting to heaven. So all the babies, small brothers and sisters of my friends, who had died before they had had a chance of baptism spent eternity in a place called Limbo. I was confronted with the unanswerable Christian question – if God were loving, how could He allow this?

Occasionally one of the parish priests would take us for Christian Doctrine especially if we were dealing with the sixth and ninth commandments and the notion of purity. Impurity was such a frightening sin. It came upon you unawares, in an impure thought – perhaps from looking at impure pictures in a magazine. Or worse still you could cause impure thoughts in others by wearing clothes that were immodest. Strapless evening gowns were appallingly dangerous. I was very impressed when Fleur asked Father, 'What are the erogenous zones?' I had never heard of them and Father's reaction indicated that he wished he'd never heard of them either. 'Ask Sister Marie Therese in your next class with her,' he said. We knew Sister Marie Therese could cope with anything.

I was more attracted to the Christian Doctrine lessons that focussed on the spiritual rather than the moral, the meaning of prayer, the awareness of God's presence, knowing that He was near us and that He truly cared for us. God became very real but I wavered between loving Him as a friend, and fearing Him as an unsmiling father-figure who would never be pleased no matter what I did. The thought that God loved me was never impressed upon me as heavily as the idea that I had to love Him. And this was something which I had to show Him, as my mother often told me, by what I did, not by what I said.

We were often told to pray to know our vocation in life.

God had a plan for all of us. It would be one of three states: single blessedness, the married state or, best of all, the life of complete dedication to God as a religious sister. We should pray daily that we would know what God wanted us to do. For if we knew and didn't choose it we would most definitely be unhappy. In forms three and four I didn't really think of becoming a nun. But I certainly didn't want to be unhappy either. As boarders we were encouraged but never forced to go to morning mass in the cathedral or in the nuns' chapel. The power of the example of the seniors getting up every morning was very strong and most of us joined them. Morning mass in the cathedral had a quiet dignity about it. I could kneel anywhere and my devotion was private.

After breakfast and tidying up the dormitory we boarders moved over to the day school. Every lesson began with a prayer and then we sat down. Unlike our primary school, St Dominic's had different teachers for different subjects. Christian Doctrine was the most important lesson but we certainly learned more than this subject. Sister Augustine took us for science classes in the science lab with gas burners and taps that could squirt water out at most unlikely angles. We learned about nutrition and the bones in the human skeleton. We learned how the amoeba spent its day and how flowers reproduced, but in the 1950s we learnt very little about our own reproductive system. We learned History in forms three and four from a textbook that was very selective. It started with Nebuchadnezzar and the Babylonian captivity, then the early days of Christianity – the martyrs singing hymns in the Roman colosseum while they were being ripped apart by lions – and progressed to the Middle Ages and the history of Religious Orders. Sister Marie Therese taught us Latin most efficiently – *amo, amas, amat, amamus, amatus, amant* – AGAIN! – *amo, amas, amat ...*' Mother Patricia taught us to be observant – 'What is the third picture from the left on the back wall?' she would ask. 'Do not look round – you see it every day. Make your mind remember.' We were not to take these works of art for granted. But some did not require such close scrutiny. There were large volumes of art prints in the school library but all nudes were delicately 'dressed' with superimposed fig leaves. I had quite a botanical view of male genitalia for many years. In form five Sister Josephine started English by writing on the board – 'I caught this morning morning's minion, king- / dom of daylight's dauphin, dapple-dawn drawn Falcon, in his riding / Of the rolling level underneath him steady air ...' 'Can you explain these lines, girls?' We looked totally blank. It sounded beautiful when she read it but what did it mean?

At least once a term each class would put on a tableau – the curtains would be drawn on the hall stage and there we would be, motionless Greeks minus the heifer, illustrating Keats's 'Ode to a Grecian Urn'. We would be dressed exactly as the figures on the Attic vase and learned to stand absolutely still for five minutes without giggling while someone recited the ode. Many of these tableaux came from set pieces in Mamour books three and four, or from *Realms of Gold*. I especially liked the one of Milton dictating *Paradise Lost* to his dutiful daughters. In this way we learned that a picture was worth a thousand words.

On 4 August we celebrated St Dominic's Day. The refectory

would be decorated with crêpe paper the night before. We would sing a special mass in the Sisters' chapel at seven and then have honey and oranges as an extra treat for breakfast. The day would be devoted to fun and games, including a basketball match in the afternoon between the senior A team and an ex-pupils' team. And then we got ready for the fancy dress ball held in Rosary Hall in the evening. The head girl was always dressed as St Dominic and carried an arum lily. But there were not many restrictions on the rest of us – we were dressed as rugby teams, suffragettes, or the nine muses. Each one of us was presented to Bishop Kavanagh, our invited guest, who always seemed rather nonplussed by the whole occasion.

Sometime each year at seven o'clock of a winter's evening there would be great chatter and laughter from the boarders' parlour. 'The debutantes are here!' A dizzy excitement pervaded the Study Hall as last year's seniors, now ex-pupils, made their debut into 'social life' by being presented to Bishop Kavanagh at the Town Hall Charity Ball. It was an old custom that they would come to the Priory first and introduce their partners to the Sisters. Fleur and I made frequent trips to the toilet next door to the parlour so that we could catch a glimpse of these amazing partners. Then the inlaid doors of the Study Hall were opened and the debutantes entered in their beautiful dresses and curtseyed to us while the nuns entertained their partners in the parlour. We crowded around, oohing and aahing at the splendour of it all.

In 1954 I was made senior boarder and relished the responsibility and limelight. I became a sort of older sister to an extended family of about forty-eight. However, Mother

Gertrude and I did not have the sort of close relationship one expects to find between senior pupils and their teachers. She remained a remote person, a perfectionist, although an inspiring singing teacher to our fine boarders' choir. We practised and practised and practised until with great personal satisfaction we knew it was right. That kind of choral singing was extremely satisfying as we were all working together to create one beautiful sound. No voice was ever allowed to dominate. I always sang alto and Mother Gertrude once said, 'You have to have brains to sing alto as you are listening as well as singing.' Rare praise indeed.

In my school career I won several prizes; one was Best Actress, which caused my father to fall about helplessly in the living room when I told him. I also won the prize for Amiability, awarded by the votes of the pupils. In my two final years I was both Dux and winner of the Christian Doctrine medal; this meant that my name could be emblazoned twice on the Honours board in the Study Hall. Mother Angela had told us that those on this board either became nuns or left the Church. Could one do both?

At the end of each term a great wave of excitement would build up in the boarding school. We would pack our cases the night before and total chaos would descend after breakfast. 'North girls, please hurry. Central, your taxi's on the way.' And we would fall into taxis clutching our hats and scarves and move off to the grandeur of the Dunedin railway station. On the last Sunday of the school year we had a splendid Christmas dinner with enormous plum puddings. Inside them the Sister in charge of the kitchen had put sixpences, rings and beads;

sixpence meant you were going to be wealthy, a ring meant marriage and the bead meant you would become a nun. Several boarders were known to have swallowed the last, but by the time I found a carefully placed bead in mine in December 1954 I knew where I was going.

# CHAPTER 5

# INITIATION

ABOUT form six I began to wish I'd been born a Protestant. There was a nagging thought in my mind which wouldn't go away that if I really loved God I should think of becoming a nun. Protestants never had such a choice. They just got married. I wanted to get married too one day but if God had a plan for me, then I would only be happy if I carried it out. And it seemed that the more I fought such an idea, the more genuine it was. After all 'The Hound of Heaven' was all about such a fight. I really identified with that poem. I'd found it in a book in the library – 'I fled Him down the nights and down the days;/ I fled Him down the arches of the years;/ I fled Him down the labyrinthine ways of my own mind.'

I didn't tell anyone about what I was fighting. Fleur had no such confusion. She left school in my form six year and would come to visit with great stories of all her new boyfriends. Life for her was exciting. I enjoyed my form seven year – it was called then Six A. There were only about five of us in the class and that year I studied English and History, both of which I loved, French whose grammar I never mastered, and Latin and Greek. I had started Greek that year and while I loved writing its alphabet I found it infinitely harder than Latin.

I used to go to confession to Father Hussey, the boarding school chaplain. He had an enormous influence on my teenage years. He was a kind, sane man with a delightful sense of humour. He kept things in proportion, often telling me I had a very sensitive conscience. Once I tentatively said after my sordid list of sins that I kept thinking of becoming a nun, probably a Carmelite. Confession is of course supposedly anonymous – a grill in a wall separates the penitent in the darkened cubicle from the Father Confessor in the other. But Father Hussey knew my voice. There was a long pause. 'Judith,' he said, 'I don't really see you keeping the silence for days on end as a Carmelite. What about a teaching order?'

The Carmelites had attracted me because they were the strictest order I knew about. There was a convent in Christchurch and the twenty-three nuns there never came out nor were seen by lay people. If they needed medical or dental attention, the doctor and the dentist went to them. They were regarded as the prayer house of the Church and if anyone had any worry or anxiety they would visit the Carmelites and ask them to pray for them. My mother had taken me there once and I had been impressed with the ritual of contact with the nuns. We had rung a bell, a door had opened into a sparse room and a soft, disembodied voice from behind a grill had said, 'God bless you. What can we do for you?' My mother had a book for the Mother Superior and when she asked for her there was a mysterious rustle, the sound of feet quietly going down corridors, doors opening and shutting and footsteps returning. Mother Superior knew my mother, warmly welcomed her, and then a sort of hole in the wall appeared for the book to be passed through. I could see no one, and I was longing to, for I knew that these Sisters wore sandals all year round and a heavy serge habit. They didn't teach or nurse – they worked in the garden, baked altar breads and above all, prayed. They lived a life of complete penance. I had decided that if I was going to be a nun I might as well pick the hardest, most disciplined Order I knew. And here was my Father Confessor quietly giggling about my choice.

'Why don't you join the Order you know best?' he said. 'You could be a very good teacher, and the Dominicans are as prayerful an Order as the Carmelites.' In a way I was relieved. I hated change and I was scared of leaving St Dominic's. The thought of going to university, meeting new people, moving into new accommodation, freedom, change if you like, terrified me. If I became a Dominican nun, I could stay in this secure, predictable environment. I looked at my teachers with more discernment. I didn't like any one of them more than any other. They were a fine group of women, all very different in personality, yet all working obviously for the same end.

In the August holidays I broached the subject with my parents. My mother was overjoyed. She regretted not becoming a Sister herself and her great wish was to 'return her children to God as pure as they were when born'. I fear we may have all failed her there. My father was far more reserved and cautious. 'I wouldn't stop you, but I don't think it's you. You can give it a try, and remember there is always a home for you here.'

I was troubled by his misgivings. He knew me well. When I told Mother Patricia, an older nun whom I'd always trusted, she said that his reactions were perfectly natural, that most parents were appalled at their children entering an Order or the priesthood. After all, they were making a sacrifice too. I was reassured. I wrote a formal letter of application on October the seventh to enter the Order and on the eleventh Mother Prioress General wrote that I had been accepted. I told Father Hussey. He looked at me and said, 'You have made the most important decision of your life and the greatest sacrifice a human being can make. Well done, Judith.' I felt I had been canonised. I began to tell a few of my school friends – some were appalled, some were amazed. I began indeed to feel I was moving away from them – I felt different, special, called by God.

The Dominicans were founded by the Spaniard, Dominic Guzman of Calaroga, in the thirteenth century. Their popular claim to fame is that they provided prosecution personnel for the Inquisition. But the Order has done much more attractive work in the Church. This was the post-Black Death period in Europe and there were too few educated priest preachers. Dominic and his followers were religious innovators, forsaking the regulated life of the cloisters to preach Christ and the gospels all over Europe. They moved from city to city and set up monasteries in Spain, France and Italy, especially in university towns. They attracted young men of recognised intellect like Thomas Aquinas, Jordan of Saxony and Albert the Great. St Thomas More had had a Dominican confessor. They fought for the intellect of people in the same way their colleagues, the Franciscans, fought for people's values. Dominic and Francis of Assisi knew each other well. Women too wanted to join Dominic but they could not become itinerant preachers. Instead, they formed convents and concentrated on educating young women. Their convents were set up all over Europe and it was from Ireland in 1871 that Mother Gabriel Gill brought her group of teaching sisters to Dunedin at the request of Bishop Moran. Foundress's Day was always celebrated in February. The Motherhouse of the Dominican Sisters in New Zealand was St Dominic's Priory and this was where I was to enter on 1 February, 1955. I was seventeen years old and had from December to February to see the world.

It was a very strange time. Unlike other holidays, this was not a time I felt I could relax. My mother decided I needed a trip, so she, Marian and I went off to Kawau Island for a week. It was a farewell to the world I barely knew, but all I wanted to do was to get on with leaving it. The last Christmas at home was wonderful and sad and every present was holy. I had to collect all my clothes for the 'trousseau' – all white underwear, yards of bleached and unbleached cotton for petticoats, black shoes and stockings, and (inexplicably) large white men's handkerchiefs, a dressing gown of sober colour, plain white nightgowns – all new, all neatly packed. My sister Gillian, going into form six flew back to Dunedin with me. This time I knew I would never see home again and I cried most of the flight down. Father Hussey met us at the airport and drove us in to the cathedral presbytery to see Bishop Kavanagh.

Both men tried very hard to make me laugh but I was very weepy. I think I 'entered' at 7pm. Gillian returned to the boarding school and I had my first view of the 'nuns' part' – rooms I'd always wanted to see when I was a boarder. There were six of us – Hazel, one or two years older, Gloria, sixteen years old and straight from Falls Road, Belfast, Joan and Pat from Invercargill who like me had just left school, and Roxane, a graduate from Training College. This was the group I would train with. We put on the black, short skirt, blouse and short veil of the postulant and met the Novice Mistress, Mother Mary Tarcisius.

She was a small and gentle lady who was to prepare us in five years of training for our Final Profession. Mother Tarcisius was a saintly soul, prayerful, and very serious about her responsibilities. Whenever she found us behaving in an un-nunly way her favourite phrase, uttered from the depths of despair was, 'Sister, I tremble for the future of the Order.'

We were taken over to the novitiate, the three-storeyed concrete building in the middle of the convent block, to meet the novices and Temporary Professed Sisters, about twenty-five in all. In most religious orders each candidate had to undergo a postulancy of nine months, not leading a nun's life fully but being observed for suitability. One could be sent home or could go home at any time – it was a kind of apprenticeship. At the end of this period the candidate formally asked the Sisters of the Order to accept her and, if accepted, the candidate prepared for her formal Reception of the Habit. She then became a novice and undertook total spiritual training for one year, being involved in no other work at all. At the end of this year she again asked the community to accept her for Temporary Profession for a period of three years, and, if accepted, she would take her three vows of poverty, chastity and obedience. In this period she could continue with secular studies, do some teaching and generally be trained mentally and spiritually for Final Profession when the three vows were taken for life.

I did not realise until I went through into the nuns' enclosure just how different my life would be. The first thing I noticed was how bare everything was. In the boarders' building there were pictures on the walls of the stairwell. Here there were none. Four flights of bare stairs went up to the top floor. They looked more like outside steps with their metal bannisters and wire grilles. Mother Tarcisius showed us our bedrooms – only they weren't bedrooms, they were called cells. They were partitioned each from the next but the walls did not go right up to the ceiling, so we could hear but not see our neighbours. Gloria clutched my arm. 'Holy Saint Joseph!' she said with horror, under her breath. In the cubicles of the boarding school we had mirrors and hand-basins and we could make our rooms personal with pictures of our family. But here there was nothing but the polished wooden floor, a narrow bed with a horsehair mattress, grey blankets, one pillow and a pure white bedspread. Each cell had a small window which opened only slightly, and was painted over white, so you felt like Macbeth, 'cribbed, cabinned and confined'. There was a wooden table and chair, a cupboard and a plain enamelled jug in a stand. The only ornament on the wall was a crucifix.

# CHAPTER 6

# ELECTED SILENCE

THE novitiate was my home for the next three years. It was a training centre, much I guess like the army or police. It wasn't long before I began to feel the contradictions inherent in the life of a nun – we were to live a life of love, of God first and above all else, and then of love for all those we worked with. Love to me implied warmth, spontaneity and generosity, but these qualities were often suppressed. For our training involved 'death to self' – a disciplined self-control of all such feelings.

We were trained to walk with our eyes down, never to draw attention to ourselves by making a noise, to kneel when we were corrected and not to make any excuse if we were blamed for something, even if it wasn't our fault. I was immediately told to quieten my laugh and my conversation. 'Wherever you are, Sister,' Mother Tarcisius said, trembling for the future of the Order, 'there's always noise.' Once I came into a room and noticed a fresh rose in a vase by a statue of Our Lady. I instinctively went over and smelled it, and I was quietly and quickly corrected for being sensual. For me, love and death to self presented a dichotomy that could never be reconciled.

Just getting used to the physical changes of our daily life was hard enough in the beginning. Personal cleanliness was achieved with great speed. Life as a boarder was regulated by the clock, but here it seemed regulated by a stop watch. At the end of each central corridor in the novitate building were about three bathrooms, lavatories and hand basins. Most of us washed ourselves here publicly one after another rather than fill a jug and splash privately back in the cell. This had to be done in about ten minutes so that we could be dressed and in the chapel in time for mass. I had always loved the chapel, often affectionately called the Wedding Cake, with its decorated altar and ceiling, its polished wooden floor, the beautiful wooden stalls for each Sister, and the green carpet runner down the middle and under the stalls, which was changed to a rich red Axminster whenever there was a first class feast. We six postulants were given our places in the chapel and were told which of the daily services we were to attend. We were 'on honeymoon' for the first month, which meant we were not required to follow the daily demanding routine. We could also make mistakes and they would be overlooked.

Mother Tarcisius showed us through the long and sunny glass cloister beside the garden with its magnificent pear tree, down the circular stairs and to the nuns' refectory. This was a dark, sunless room where all our meals would be taken. There was a huge crucifix on one wall and the only windows faced the archway cloister and were made opaque with white paint. There was a lectern, for all meals were eaten in silence while a Sister read aloud. The scrubbed deal tables were set in a large square with a centre table for the novices and postulants, under the watchful eye of everyone else. The Sisters sat in order of their profession and status – Mother Prioress General and Mother Prioress at the top table, with the four Mother Councillors next. At the bench end of this room there was a small table jammed beside the dishmaster and under the Zip. This was for the three or four lay Sisters.

This shocked most of us. We were New Zealanders, born and bred into an egalitarian society, yet here were women old enough to be our grandmothers who were the lowest of all the hierarchy. They had their Recreation in a separate room next to the kitchen and cellars, and took their places in the chapel and everywhere else behind us young recruits. The lay Sisters were uneducated women who had chosen to enter knowing that they would do the menial work of the convent and they dressed differently, wearing a black scapular instead of the choir Sisters' cream one. The work the lay Sisters did in the Order was the work that all housewives do, and the Order's attitude was a hangover from Victorian times. Lay Sisters were separated from choir Sisters until the early 1960s when no new postulants were accepted as lay Sisters, and all Sisters who entered after 1956 were asked to sign a document that they would do whatever work the Order required of them, be it teaching or cooking or caring for the sick in the convent infirmary. But it took some time for me to forget the annoyance of a particular choir Sister who found herself receiving Holy Communion alongside a lay Sister.

I looked around the refectory with awe and then Mother Tarcisius said, 'Each of you will be in charge of this refectory for a month at a time next year.' She spoke as if it were a position of some honour, but I was immediately petrified at the thought of serving meals, setting tables and washing dishes for 52 people – all in a limited time, and all in silence.

A difficult concept for lay people to grasp is that the life of a nun can be extremely stressful. Those images of serene faces, unhurried gait and peaceful other-worldliness that Hopkins's 'Heaven Haven' and the popular 'Nuns' Chorus' convey are not real. We who were working for eternal life fought with time from the moment we were wakened. The rising bell was rung in all buildings of the convent at 5.30am. No one was allowed to rise before it except those with special duties, like the Infirmarian. Lights went off at 10pm. It was a long and hard day and every minute of it was accounted for. We postulants were not called until 6.30am, although it was impossible to sleep through the rising bell. We had twenty-five minutes to wash and dress, pull back our beds for airing and go down to the chapel where we joined the rest of the community for mass. This lasted until 7.40 when we processed to the refectory for breakfast. At 8am we returned to the chapel for private prayers until 8.10 when we made our beds, mopped out the cell and did housework until 9am.

My job that first month was to sweep, dust and polish four flights of stairs. 'I'll never finish that by nine,' I said in amazement to the senior novice. 'Yes you will,' she said shortly. 'You have to.' So I sprinkled the damp tea leaves on each step to stop the dust, and went at it like the chase sequence of a Benny Hill show. The brooms then had to be cleaned and stored, broom head up, dusters folded and each of us took our places quietly, if sweatily, in the novitiate round the large square table for our first training session with Mother Tarcisius.

What did we learn? We learnt to sing Gregorian chant, the purest form of singing. The simplicity and beauty of this sound encapsulated the ideal of religious life for me – a pure, selfless joy in the service of God. I delighted in voicing those soul-piercing, unaccompanied melodies, letting the notes rise and fall 'like a chiffon scarf' as Mother would say. Gregorian chant still moves me easily to tears and I found it sad that the Church reforms moved away from that form of worship to communal hymn-singing often accompanied by guitars. We have lost a great deal of the awe and 'otherness' of worship in our attempt to make it accessible. Most of us had read Latin at school and we learnt to translate all the official prayers of the Church, known as 'the Divine Office' while we were in the novitiate. The Divine Office consisted of eight sections. We sang the morning 'Hours' of Prime, Terce, Sext and None before mass. Vespers was at 5pm and the lovely last 'hour' of the day, Compline, was sung in the evening. As postulants we attended only Vespers and Compline. I grew to love the plaintive sound of the prayer *In manus tuas, Domine, commendo spiritum meum* and the piercing sweetness of the 'Salve Regina' which ended Compline. Most of the office was chanted on one note – G – by alternate sides of the choir, but Compline was always sung to its liturgically set melodies and they were very beautiful.

We also learnt the rules of the religious life as set down very early on in Church history by Saint Augustine of Hippo. We had to memorise this translation and also learn the

Constitution of the New Zealand Dominican Sisters, a plain black book of rules with a rather negative tone. It was Mother Tarcisius's mission to mould us into Dominican Sisters while supposedly retaining the best of our individuality. We had to learn the practical meaning of the three vows we would take – poverty (owning nothing); chastity (owning nobody and giving all our love to Christ and his people); and obedience (negating our own will to the common good). Learning to live in community wasn't too difficult after boarding school but there was for me a self-consciousness about the novitiate that I had never felt before. I was now consciously trying to be a better person as were all the novices and postulants. As a boarder I only thought of being a better person if I was confronted by Mother Gertrude in a session in the Mistress of Schools' room.

Detachment from our families and friends was very painful. We had given these up to follow Christ. I knew all the boarders who lived in the adjacent building, but I was forbidden to communicate with them in any way. I'd be walking down a corridor on duty in school and suddenly a chattering, cheerful bunch of sixth formers would converge. 'Hello, Judith – what's it like?' And I couldn't ever respond. I had to keep my eyes lowered and move on quickly. Once I was sent to help the boarders' choir sing at a feast day mass – 'They need strength in the altos,' Mother Tarcisius had said. I was standing right beside them singing, but I might as well have been a singing lamp post. She praised me for my self-discipline but I hated it. Even more stifling was the hour I was allowed to spend with my sister Gillian on the fourth Sunday of every month, except during Lent and Advent. We sat like church mice in the grandeur of the boarders' parlour and whispered to each other.

'Do you like it?'

'I think so.'

'What's the food like?'

'Good.'

I wasn't allowed to gossip, to reveal any details of life in the cloister – all my conversation had to be 'edifying'. Gillian didn't really want to be edified. She would talk about school but wanted to know more about my new life. I felt I was being cut in half. One part of me wanted to talk like mad, like the old days, to Gill; the other knew I had a new responsibility, a new self-discipline I had to enforce. It was a painful hour, like going to a funeral once a month, and both of us were glad when it was over.

Writing letters home once a week was worse. We sat in the novitiate and wrote at the big polished table in silence – to Mum and Dad – in Ireland or Christchurch or Invercargill. Again the letters had to be edifying and they were always read by the Novice Mistress before they were posted. There wasn't much news to tell of a week's exciting adventures in the novitiate. So mine became mini sermons. 'Next Saturday is the feast of The Holy Rosary. Do you still say the Rosary at home together? I hope so because, as Father Peyton says, "The family that prays together stays together".' Or, 'We are about to go into Lent and I know you will all be giving up something you really like in order to show God you truly love Him' – and this to my parents!

At 1pm and at 5.30pm, and from 8pm till 9, we had Recreation. In spite of the rule that we weren't to have 'particular' friends and should sit beside somebody different each night, I really enjoyed these sessions. There was a lot of laughing and teasing and noise. I learnt to admire the quick wit of the Irish Sisters and I loved their accent. They were a warm, feisty lot and I knew they had given up a great deal more than we New Zealanders in entering this convent. There were about twenty-five of us, all from different families and backgrounds and I didn't dislike anyone. Nevertheless, in mid-March I suddenly got inexplicably homesick. Mother Tarcisius used to give out the mail at the one o'clock Recreation and my mother's letter had something in it about our old, much-loved cat, Ebony. I started to cry and Mother Tarcisius moved in firmly. A sacrifice was a sacrifice. I had left home. Look at all the Irish Sisters cheerfully flying miles away from home to serve God. It worked. I pulled myself together. I would never again cry in public.

Each of us was given a senior novice to be our 'angel' in the first few months. Mine was Sister Perpetua, a little Irish body, immensely kind and warm. She told me how she and her friends, Sister Jacinta and Sister Marie de Lourdes, had been recruited eighteen months before by Mother Philomena to work in New Zealand. Much had been made of the snow-capped mountains, the green hills and the clear streams. Mother Philomena was by way of being a poet. They honestly believed they were coming to some island paradise to teach the natives. I'm pleased that they stayed here even though their eventual pupils were not what they expected. While we talked at Recreation, our hands were busy mending our clothes, sewing on name tapes or embroidering endless numbers of tray cloths. These latter were often given as thank-you gifts to the convent doctor or tradesmen.

I began tertiary study while I was a postulant. Being a member of an enclosed Order, which meant the nuns did not go outside the convent walls except in cases of emergency, I could not attend university in person. I studied Latin I and Greek I extramurally. I was very lucky to have Mary Hussey as my Latin tutor. She was Father Hussey's older sister and had been to St Dominic's with my mother. My mother spoke of her with awe as being a brilliant scholar. She was also an extremely modest and shy person. I enjoyed working with her on Cicero's *Pro Caelio* – we had a lot of fun with the line, 'O, immoderata mulier!' She made Latin live for me in those hourly sessions after tea. I also taught music. I had passed my Trinity College senior exams while a boarder but now I had to become a competent teacher for all the non-examination music pupils the Sisters taught – 'The Robin's Return' and 'Remembrance' ones. Because we could not attend Training College in those days, we studied for our teachers' 'C' examinations extramurally through the Correspondence School. It was a very busy year.

But for all that there was in me a nagging unhappiness that never went away. It didn't seem to be just homesickness. I wasn't as happy as I thought I ought to be. 'Happiness is a by-product – you won't find it by looking for it,' my Father Confessor used to say if ever I asked him about it. I was ashamed to admit I wasn't happy. Was I just being selfish?

I was supposed to be making a sacrifice – surely I realised that this life would be difficult. I looked at the others in the novitiate often, mentally comparing my attitude with what I thought was theirs. They seemed to just get on with life. They looked happy too, in an unconscious way. I was told I was too introspective, too proud perhaps. 'Forget yourself in the service of others.'

It didn't work. Three months after I'd entered I followed Mother Tarcisius into the novitiate kitchenette where the altar breads for mass were baked, and burst into tears. She was very concerned and closed the door behind us.

'I want to go home,' I said, bleakly.

# CHAPTER 7

# 'GOD LOVES YOU SPECIALLY'

THEORETICALLY a novice or a postulant could leave the Order at any time. I had very mixed feelings when I told Mother Tarcisius how I felt. I was a failure and I didn't like that. I didn't think my mother would be too impressed if I returned home. And yet I didn't feel 'right' in the convent. Mother Tarcisius listened gravely. She told me I was making up my mind too soon, that three months into a new lifestyle often brought things to a crisis. Wouldn't I try for a little longer? When I said that no one else seemed to be feeling like me, she gave a reply I couldn't argue with. 'God loves you, perhaps, especially – possibly more than He does the others. Maybe He is asking more of you than He is of the others. He is testing you – can you refuse Him?' It was an appeal on her part to my generosity, but I saw it as a personal challenge – God loved me especially. There is such a thing as spiritual pride and I suffered from it. Now I could be both a martyr and a saint, and I consoled myself with that. So I started again, feeling I was especially chosen, hand-picked for greater things.

The rest of the year of postulancy was involved with passing academic exams as well as spiritual ones. But there were fun times too – impromptu picnics on a feast day if the weather was good. We would be called to the novitiate at 9am and told to get lunches organised and be ready for the cars at 9.30 to go to Santa Sabina, the convent in North East Valley. There was a large tract of bush between the convent and what is now Aquinas College university hostel, and we would be free to walk and talk and eat till about five, when we would pile back into taxis to the novitiate. It was a wonderful relaxation.

I never told any other postulant or novice of my talk to Mother Tarcisius. I was ashamed of it. I was also scared that I might give a bad example to another Sister by saying I wanted to leave. There was an unspoken loyalty to the idea of religious life that I could not betray.

But picnics were great occasions for getting rid of minor frustrations. During one blissful picnic Sister Mary said, 'I feel so mad I just want to scream.' 'Do,' I said casually. And then we had to shut her up smartly after an ear-piercing shriek that suggested murder and rape to the whole of North Dunedin. She said she felt a whole lot better. Generally though no one lost her self-control or temper. The most frequent outburst, and one which was fatal in that rigidly disciplined set-up, was the giggles. They could happen in chapel where we were kneeling in silence and someone's stomach would start rumbling. It sounded deafening and I often had to pinch myself hard or drop my handkerchief to stop shaking. Or the organist, giving us the note to intone the antiphon at Compline, would mistakenly play it two octaves too high and there would be a breathless pause before the first chantress found the right note. Or when one of the old or deaf Sisters suffered a bout of flatulence each time she genuflected during the fourteen stations of the cross. Or when Sister Margaret came down to mass minus part of her head-dress and had to be discreetly shepherded away. (It was easy to do since you could not check yourself in a mirror.)

The novices, being young, were expected to provide entertainment for the Priory Sisters on big feast days. We wrote satires and skits and sometimes did imitations of well-known ecclesiastics. Sister Annette, who entered a year or so after I did and was a close friend from boarding school was not just an excellent pianist but a marvellous mimic, and she could do Bishop Kavanagh – shy, gentle Bishop Kavanagh – to a 'T'. Mother Prioress General loved that. We also had to act out incidents from the Gospel or the lives of the saints and these were more memorable for the unintentional hilarity they inspired than their devotion. Sister Bernadine ruined a morality play about the infant Christ when she saluted Him, 'O Babe divine!' in Marilyn Monroe tones. One Easter the whole community went to the junior classroom where the curates from the cathedral presbytery gave us a spirited version of 'The Banana Boat Song'. I'd never heard such a marvellous rhythm, and Sister Annette and I were in ecstasy.

Postulants and novices were also the school and convent cleaners along with the lay Sisters. Once the pupils left we swept and polished floors, pushing cumbersome wooden blocks with wooden handles over folded pieces of blanket until the waxed floors shone like glass. We cleaned toilets and handbasins and windows and floors and light shades, and polished brass and silver until the whole room glowed and smelled with that peculiar wax smell that convent classrooms exuded. I never lay awake in that hard little bed at night and could not concentrate for more than a minute on the Four Last Things I was supposed to consider – Death, Judgment, Heaven and Hell.

I actually began teaching that year as a postulant when I was sent to standard two class at St Joseph's School to let the Sister teacher have her lunch at noon. I was told to take her class of thirty young girls and boys for elocution, a safe subject for a beginner. These were a spritely bunch of youngsters who took a fair bit of controlling, but it didn't put me off. I caught the ability to teach from watching others who were very good at it and who disciplined, not ever by yelling. 'If there's a great deal of noise in the classroom, the teacher is probably making most of it,' we were told. So I learnt to stare long and hard at a miscreant, I learnt to stop mid-sentence if someone was whispering. It was all so easy in classrooms in 1955 when the expectation was that students would want to learn.

Then in October we six postulants were called to the Chapter Room, where we asked permission of the choir Sisters to receive the Habit of the Order. I still had serious doubts about my attitude, but the Order was pleased to accept all of us and, as Mother Tarcisius pointed out to me, I wasn't meant to like what I was doing. A sacrifice was a sacrifice after all. We were now to undergo one year of rigorous spiritual training.

The ceremony where we received the habit was a public one held in the chapel in front of our families and invited guests. The ceremony was very sentimental. We were first dressed as brides of Christ (our parents having to provide the wedding dresses) and processed into the chapel, each of us with our flower girls. My sister Marian, then aged seven, was mine. Mother Prioress General, sitting in front of the altar, symbolically reminded us that we had renounced the world and all its glory by cutting a lock from our hair. She then gave us our habits. We processed out with these, quickly changed into the cumbersome and very new clothes and made our way carefully back into the chapel looking now like nuns. It was a visual shock for our families. Several parents took out handkerchiefs and cried quietly. But the family photos taken round St Dominic's statue in the convent gardens later exuded joy and pride in fulfilling a Catholic ambition to give one's child to the Church.

It was certainly unpleasant for 1950s girls to have to put on so many long layers. Over our normal white underwear went the long, calico petticoat – unbleached bodice, long sleeves and a bleached full skirt with three wide hems in honour of the Holy Trinity. Then came the cream serge under-sleeves which were safety-pinned onto the calico sleeves of the petticoat. We put on the habit next, a voluminous, long-sleeved, full-length tunic in cream serge which was gathered round the waist with a thick, black, leather belt from which hung the full rosary beads. We were to learn to walk so that these did not disturb the silence. (Crashing the beads against the choir stalls was a grave misdemeanour and breach of silence.) On top of this went the Dominican scapular which, as its name suggested, fitted over the shoulders and fell down back and front from the neck. It covered any sign of a figure. We were to keep our hands folded behind its front panel. Worst of all to put on was the starched, white guimpe, or wide bib, which was held in place by two straps covering our ears and pinned together on the crown of our head as if we had the mumps. The actual head-dress with its starched white wings, forehead band, and attached white veil went on last. We had no mirrors and all this had to be put on very quickly in the mornings. We were totally encased in this outfit for the rest of our lives.

It was a great relief to take these clothes off at night, but even in bed our heads were covered with a soft bonnet. When we took our first vows a year later, our heads were shaved like Buddhist monks, mostly for reasons of hygiene. It was a hideous sight to see my reflection in the bathroom window, much more effective in its *memento mori* than Hamlet's remarks over Yorick's skull.

We had to make our own habits, and that was a nightmare for me. I had never been good at sewing and to machine these long, straight lines of bulky material together was something I dreaded. I had to unstitch so much but luckily my friends took pity on me and frequently rescued my despairing efforts in the sewing room. We each had two habits and we wore these outer garments for a month at a time, having to keep them scrupulously unspotted. This was almost impossible and worse, the smell of perspiration that exuded from us after we had polished floors was not the sort of odour of sanctity I had expected. Deodorants and talcum powder were of course worldly and unnecessary toiletries.

When we did our cleaning duties we had to 'tuck up' – that

is, pull the habit skirt up around our waist and hold it together with a large safety pin at the back. A priest once pointed out how strange it was seeing women walking around with their petticoats in full view. The wearing of the habit was, of course, a penance. I had renounced the world with all its finery and I truly found wearing this dress a hardship. But on the outside at least I looked like a nun.

# Chapter 8

# A White Novice

IF I had wanted to be a Carmelite, my year as a white novice should have been a joy. After our nine months of postulancy we received the habit but wore a white veil instead of the black one to show that we were still in training. We were called 'white novices'. We were to be entirely 'enclosed' – that is, to have no contact with any secular person and to concentrate instead on our spiritual development. The goal was Temporary Profession, taking the three vows of poverty, chastity and obedience for three years. The six of us had to be trained for one year by the Novice Mistress in canon law as it applied to religious life, in the history of the Order, in spirituality and in self-discipline. We were not side-tracked by any secular study either for university or training college.

Now I got up in the morning with the rising bell at 5.30am. The Divine Office was chanted from 6 till 6.30. It was, we were taught, the public prayer of the Church sung in monastic choirs all over the world, a set ritual of hymns, psalms and readings from the Old and New Testaments and the lives of the saints. All of our work was interlaced with prayer, either public or private. Every day was devoted to a saint from the Church's calendar or to a seasonal reflection from the Church's liturgical year.

Much of the Second Nocturn biographies we read as part of Matins were of an edifying nature – sometimes bordering on the laughable. Was it, for instance, piety, when the infant Thomas Aquinas ate paper with the words of the Hail Mary on it – wouldn't any eight-month-old have done the same? But certain human elements surfaced in these readings and I had my favourite saints. I have always loved Saint Thomas More, the man who could mix with anyone, the most human of all saints who never lost his sense of humour or proportion in his total loyalty to Christ. The fact that he tried religious life and then realised it was not his calling made him even more of a friend. I admired Saint Margaret of Hungary for her generosity to others in spite of her husband's remonstrances. I was also drawn to the gentleness of Saint Francis de Sales and the common sense of Saint Teresa of Avila. I especially liked her remark to Christ – 'Lord, if this is the way you treat your friends, no wonder you have so few'.

Mother Tarcisius took us for about three lectures a day in the novitiate. We sat round the long, oak table while she read or commented on some spiritual writing to us. She was especially fond of the writings of a Benedictine monk, Dom Marmion, but we also read works by Dominicans like Gerald Vann, Anselm Moynihan and Bede Jarrett. Sometimes a word or phrase seemed particularly apt or welcome and I would remember it all day. I still recall a definition of God (can one define God?) that appealed to me far more than 'God is our loving father' or 'God is the creator of the universe', or 'God became man in Christ'. It was, 'God is infinite attractiveness'.

Meditation involved a technique. Mother Tarcisius taught us to pray first for the grace to meditate well. Then we should read a short passage from the Gospels or a spiritual book of our own choice, close the book and think about it prayerfully. Every morning from 6.30 to 7.00 and fifteen minutes after tea were our designated times for meditation and I often found them the best part of the day. Here was spiritual food for the day's energy. But there were also times of depression when I could think of nothing in that half hour but 'my sweating self, and worse'. Then meditation became barren introspection. I hated myself for not getting anywhere spiritually. I would furtively look across at Sister Helena. She may have been thinking of the last race at Trentham for all I knew, but her face always had an expression of angelic sweetness. Or I battled with a tendency to go to sleep. The chapel was heated, we sat to meditate and it was our personal responsibility to do so. No one would know we were doing anything else – unless we snored. Sometimes meditation seemed only to compound my problems.

I was very attracted to the practice of recalling the 'indwelling of God'. This was where a Sister would recall at any time during the day or night that God lived within her soul and she would prayerfully acknowledge His presence. Mother taught us that we should never be so preoccupied with what we were doing that we would forget God's presence. It certainly helped to keep life in perspective. Sometimes though Mother Tarcisius caught me off guard. She was a very quiet person and could glide into a room before anyone saw her. Once when I was wrestling with the altar bread machine which kept overheating and sticking, someone suddenly said, 'Sister!' behind me. I jumped, and in a pained voice Mother remarked, 'Really, Sister, you ought to be living in the presence of God.'

Another of Mother Tarcisius's duties in this year of noviceship was to teach us the meaning, relevance and practice of the vows we would take at the end of the year. Poverty meant we owned nothing and shared everything. Actually, we wanted for nothing in the convent. Poverty trained us not to be acquisitive. If we needed new shoes or stockings or soap or toothpaste we wrote our requirements in a special notebook outside the procuratrix's office (the delicious title meant the same as bursar). In due course our needs were met. If we had to wait, so much the better for our acquisitiveness. For me poverty came to mean that nothing was permanently mine. Naturally I got used to the cell I slept in, but sometimes if we had visitors I would be told to shift to another cell. Or my stall in the chapel with my missal, breviary and spiritual reading books was changed. I hated change but I needed to keep accepting it to remind myself that 'we have not here a lasting city'. Death should have meant the final loss of all possessions but I came to like the idea of death for its immovability – at least I would be lying in the same place for ever.

The vow of chastity was a far more difficult notion to come to terms with. The key word seemed to be sublimation. We were to channel our love to the pure service of God in others. Instead of giving it all to one person we would be free to love everyone. This can work, for many nuns are known as excellent teachers, giving themselves totally to care for the children they teach. But I found it a very negative practice. I became attached to people too easily, either to other Sisters or to pupils I taught. We were not allowed to have what was called 'particular friends'. I felt this was a basic contradiction – wasn't friendship by its very nature particular? While I got on well with everyone, there were people I immediately warmed to. I realised something was going wrong when I developed an adolecent crush on Sister Ann. She was about ten years older than I was but had entered after me as a late vocation. She had a wonderful sense of humour and a far greater experience of life than I had ever had. I found her fascinating to listen to and laugh with and deliberately chose to sit near her at Recreation. For about six weeks she dominated my thoughts – I was infatuated. Then suddenly she was shifted to another convent. I was heartbroken. No one in authority said anything to me but Sister Mary, another novice, said we had become too close and it had been noticed. Out of sight, out of mind was the remedy, and it worked. I had never heard of lesbianism but it was obviously a real worry to Superiors in the Order. The treatment was always swift separation – there was no acknowledgement, no discussion, no counselling at all.

Sexual matters were never really discussed. It was presumed that we knew the facts of life but from conversations with one of the Irish Sisters, I knew she didn't. She couldn't understand her parents' outrage in their letters to her about her brother and his new wife having a baby three months after their wedding. A priest once remarked that the Sisters took little notice of the biological realities of being women. I worked out that he was talking about pre-menstrual tension – something which was totally ignored in the convent. When Mother David became Prioress General in 1957 she decided that we should know what we were giving up, so we had talks on sexual and reproductive matters. Fortuitously Sister Christopher had been both a trained nurse and midwife before she entered so she was given the job of enlightener. She did it very well. One day she was drawing the reproductive organs in detail on the blackboard when old Sister Angela walked in. 'What's that?' she demanded. 'An octopus?' And an octopus it remained. Sister Christopher had a plastic model of one of our internal organs – could it have been the oesophagus? – and she took an evil pleasure in using it as a vase in front of the many statues.

Obedience was a concept we were already accustomed to. Mostly, in the 1950s, parents expected a certain obedience from their children and in Catholic schools it was an assumed mode of behaviour. The Church itself worked in an authoritarian structure and the convent had an hierarchical order. We were numerically ranked from the date of our religious profession, unless we became Mother Prioress General. She was number one. I became number 143. In the novitiate we obeyed the Novice Mistress in everything. That year was easy as there were seldom conflicting interests, but I did find it extremely hard to obey an order to take a class for someone for the week before university exams.

We were trained to obey bells instantly even if it meant leaving a job unfinished. At 5.30am we had to get out of bed, our feet on the bare floor immediately, no few extra minutes to wake up. If we slept in someone would knock on our door with the call '*Benedicamus Domino*' to which we had to reply, '*Deo gratias*'. It was hard to thank God under those conditions. Unpunctuality was a fault because it presupposed a wilfulness of spirit as well as sloth.

It was Mother Tarcisius's job to correct us daily for these misdemeanours and she did so with gentle firmness. I really did feel she was trying to make me better. When we were corrected, we had to kneel in silence with eyes down. If the fault was serious we were reprimanded in the Chapter of Faults and given a public penance. The Chapter of Faults was held weekly in both the novitiate and later with the senior Sisters in the community room, and I can still feel the cold chill of fear that the Chapter bell summoned up in me. We sat as in choir in the community room, opposite each other and in silence. One by one, starting with the juniors, we stood out in the centre of the room, bent over and recited our faults – faults like breaking the silence 'in all its forms and on every occasion' as Sister John Baptist once admitted while we pinched ourselves to stop laughing. 'Breaking' the silence meant speaking unnecessarily during the times of silence, especially the Profound Silence from 9pm till 6am. It also meant any noise that we might make, say, in moving from one place to another. Inadvertently banging a door was breaking the silence. It was also a fault to neglect our Sisters at table. The list of petty faults went on and on and then we prostrated ourselves on the floor, face down, and waited for any further accusations. Any other Sister could stand and remind us, in complete charity of course, of other faults we had neglected to mention. This I hated, listening from my prone position to hear what horrors of misconduct I had forgotten to admit to. Self-esteem was pride, and not encouraged and the result was I felt guilty and third-rate for many years. Mother Prioress would admonish the prostrate Sister and then give a penance which was generally performed publicly in the refectory during meal times. The punishment for serious breaches of the Rule was called Cross Prayers. A Sister would rise from the table, make the 'venia' (the prostration) and then stand again and extend her arms in the form of a cross while she silently recited certain psalms. If we accidentally broke a dish or utensil our penance was to hold this up in the refectory for a minute of silent prayer as a means of begging pardon for our carelessness. When Sister Gregory broke a chamberpot while on infirmary duty, she had to hold it up during tea.

Once we became novices and received the habit we also had a change of name, like all brides at that time. We were to choose the name of a Saint we admired, join it to Mary (our Lady's name) and submit it to the community for acceptance. So Judith Hobbs became Sister Mary Stephen – a complete change of identity to go with the change of appearance. Stephen was the name of the first Christian martyr stoned to death at the behest of St Paul for his allegiance to Christ. My feast day was to be the day after Christmas. I knew very little about St Stephen, but the Greek name had an unpretentious strength about it that I much preferred to Guiseppi (suggested by Mother Tarcisius), or Frigidian or Amata – and there were Sisters with those names.

I managed to survive the novitiate, but I had long sessions in the confessional talking to various priests about how I should persevere. I had no doubt that this was where God wanted me to be for the perverse reason that I didn't want it – it was a sacrifice. No one of those I consulted ever suggested I should leave. It was a decision I should have made myself but I couldn't. I believed that God was asking me to do something special for Him and I felt I could not refuse.

# CHAPTER 9

## DEATH TO SELF

IN October 1956 we six who had entered as postulants in February 1955 were told that the Order had accepted us for Temporary Profession. No one had left and as far as I could tell (for we never talked about this) no one was going to. I seemed to be the only person who had doubts. Was I too introspective? If I could just get on with the job as all my colleagues seemed to, wouldn't I be just as happy and settled as they were? My spiritual directors kept telling me that God would give me the strength. Before our profession the six of us made a private retreat – nine days of absolute silence and reflection on what we were about to do. There is something extraordinary about a retreat – a total withdrawal from everyday living, a period of intense concentration on the spiritual. I was about to make the supreme sacrifice, 'death to self' as spiritual writers put it. All those who make retreats of this length speak of an elation of spirit which follows. My elation after this retreat was largely due to deep relief – *I had made a decision*. I may not have liked it, I may not have wanted to make it, but in doing so I had temporarily stopped the self-questioning and fruitless introspection. The photographs of that day show my relief. I was nineteen years old.

The six of us took our temporary vows in the chapel of St Dominic's on 8 December 1956. We knelt individually in front of Mother Prioress General and Bishop Kavanagh and various visiting priests and exchanged the white veil of the novice for the black veil of the professed Sister. All my family were present and Bishop Joyce of Christchurch, a friend of my father, sent down a gift and an encouraging letter. I went forward to a new life with the mind of Sydney Carton in *Tale of Two Cities* as he took his friend's place at the guillotine: 'It is a far, far better thing that I do than I have ever done'. From that day on our six lives changed dramatically.

Mother Prioress General decided that we were to be trained much more intensively for our teaching careers. She set up a Scholasticate, a room where we were to pursue our studies for the Teachers' 'C' Certificate, our extramural university units and music and speech training so that we could earn money by teaching music and elocution to private pupils. We were also put in front of classes to teach with a senior Sister as our mentor. One evening each week a lecturer from Dunedin Training College gave us lectures on child development and educational philosophy. As well as that we were taught aspects of canon law and interpretations of the Old and New Testament by the Dominican Fathers of North East Valley. It was stimulating, and also exhausting.

The room we used as a study whenever we had a free hour had once been a violin studio. It was a small, over-heated room with about five of us in there at any one time. I regularly fell asleep at my desk in the morning and eventually a senior scholasticate Sister broke the silence to say, 'You're too tired. You're overdoing it. Go and ask if you can drop your work for A.T.C.L.' I burst into tears and she made an appointment for me to see Mother Prioress General. Her office was called the Blue Room and it was situated on the third floor of the Priory buildings. If you were sent for there it was for a matter of great moment – a shift, perhaps; a telling off; a new promotion. Mother David listened to my sobs quite gravely, as she was to do many times, and told me I possibly was attempting too much in one year and, yes, I could drop my music study. I was to keep on teaching non-examination pupils though.

We were still part of the novitiate, the seniors in fact, but we felt like young adults in the family home ready to leave for the real work in other convents. By the end of 1957 the six of us had split, moving to live in suburban convents around Dunedin. Sister Denise (Roxane), for instance, went to Santa Sabina convent in North East Valley, Sister Gregory (Hazel) to Dominican Hall in Park Street. I stayed at St Dominic's but was given a great variety of teaching experience in primary classes, taking standards three and four in Study Hall with the lively and inventive Sister Cyprian. An older Sister must have become ill at Kaikorai Valley convent and I was taken up there daily to teach her infant classes for about a month. It was very strange to work in a small convent and I felt lost and ill at ease. As an outsider I was very much more aware of tensions in a convent of five Sisters and I don't know how I would have coped had I lived there instead of being just a daily visitor. But the infant class was an amazing revelation – all those small bodies wanting individual attention at the same time, so it seemed. There were the dominant, bossy ones and the shy little ones, like Moya, who had just started that week and would vomit within ten minutes of being in the classroom. She was used to being in a quiet home and found the noise of that classroom too much to cope with. She survived – and so did I, with a great respect for infant teachers. It was part of our training to spend a sizeable amount of time with every age group from beginning school through to senior secondary; an experience that proved invaluable.

In 1958 I began teaching secondary classes at St Dominic's College while half-way through my degree. I spent my days now attending university in person – a requirement for doing any stage two subjects – and teaching forms three and four in my old school. I loved the teaching. Dozens and dozens of marvellous girls who have gone on to do daring deeds – the Sandras, the Bernadettes, the Marys, the Anitas, the Wynsomes, the Elizabeths, the Janices; I loved them all.

But I was not brimming with youthful confidence in either role, as teacher or university student. I attended lectures in History II and English II and Anthropology I, the latter chosen for me simply because it was held at the convenient time of 9am. But I was not allowed to mix socially with anyone at university and could speak only in necessity to the sixth form girl who was deputed to accompany me to and from lectures. We were not permitted to travel anywhere on our own. A large part of me ached for the real university life but forgoing that was part of the sacrifice. So I slid as inconspicuously as I could in a habit, from lecture theatre to classroom and back. Sometimes I went with the other Sisters who were doing university work, if our lecture times coincided, and one of these was Sister Mary Elizabeth Mackie, a senior when I was at school and a person I always respected for her lucid intelligence, disarming honesty and great integrity. She completed a brilliant Classics degree at Otago University and was then awarded a scholarship to Somerville College in Oxford. On her return to Dunedin she was the first Dominican Sister to be appointed a lecturer in Classics. St Dominic would have loved it. She is now a very able administrator for the Council of Churches of Aotearoa, New Zealand.

About this time the Order decided on something quite momentous – the Sisters' head-dresses were to change. It was an enormous job for the Sisters who ran the laundry at Santa Sabina to starch all our guimpes and head-dresses every week. So it was decreed we should go into something simpler and softer. On the day, we were to be photographed in the old head-dresses and then change and be photographed in the new. They may not have looked so different from the old because still nothing of our hair was visible but they were a great deal more comfortable to wear. For the first few days we all felt self-conscious coming out from the wings, so to speak.

Back in the secondary classroom I was being quietly remonstrated with for being 'too open' with the girls. 'Remember, Sister, you are on a pedestal and you must never forget it.' I found it impossible to be as reserved as was expected, for teaching was above all else communication, and to communicate I had to be open, I had to be me. At the end of that first year of teaching the school was visited by state inspectors. The nuns set out to impress them totally. The entire school was cleaned twice over – windows gleamed, floors shone and the girls in these polished classrooms were drilled in how to stand and greet the inspectors. My class was not the brightest and a Mr Stan Knight came to see me teaching them. I was very nervous but eventually forgot he was there. The next day the principal, Sister Marie Therese called me in to say how pleased Mr Knight was with my teaching. Then I met him myself and the words of praise and encouragement he gave me set me up for life. I am still very grateful to both Sister Marie Therese and Mr Knight – they need not have said what they did but in doing so they set me firmly and confidently in the classroom at a job I have never ceased to love.

# CHAPTER 10

# THE EXPENSE OF SPIRIT

THE life of a white novice seemed years away now as we junior professed took our places in classrooms. I don't think I have ever been so busy or so tired. Teaching in itself is demanding but it was the before and after activities which started at 5.30am and ended at 10pm that made it so exhausting. To raise money for the school most of the convents ran fairs and St Dominic's had a two-day garden fête every October. Two Sisters were assigned to be in charge of each of the four stalls. The fête would start on Friday night in Rosary Hall and continue on Saturday, ending with a great flourish on Saturday night. Parents were wonderful, donating time and energy with almost crusader-like zeal to the school's cause.

But we also asked the business community of Dunedin for support. There is nothing worse than phoning total strangers to ask for donations and we went through the phone book taking a quarter of the listed forms each, Catholic or not. Again we met with staggering generosity. I do remember one fund-raising activity with delight. Margaret Farry was asked to bring a fashion parade to the school. She very cheerfully agreed and I was enchanted by the racks and racks of beautiful dresses that arrived on the stage at Rosary Hall. This was very worldly of me and I had to resist my attraction to the glamorous image of both the models and their dresses. That was where I saw my first television set operating in Dunedin. Mrs French, one of our superwomen helpers brought one up to Rosary Hall as part of a fundraising effort. We were stupefied. What vast areas were suddenly opened to us! It had become fashionable to run debates and speeches in classrooms on the evil of television and how it would ruin family life, but that didn't lessen its fascination.

It's amazing what connotations the words 'family life' held for me - warmth, comfort, sitting round a table eating and talking and laughing with your own. From my cell window on the second floor of the novitiate building, I would look enviously over at the two-storeyed white stuccoed house opposite in Rattray Street and watch the family at a meal or sitting round in front of a fire. I was miffed when they pulled the curtains. Family life was what I secretly wanted and the renunciation of it got harder by the day. The thought of loving one person totally was always attractive. The only young men around were the cathedral curates who came to say daily mass for us in the chapel. They were fine men, courteous, kind and often very funny but we really had very little to do with them in spite of all the rumours about secret tunnels connecting the Priory and the Presbytery. I'd been looking for them for years... Many of the curates had impressive singing voices and the cathedral services for Holy Week were not just a spiritual but also a cultural highlight for me. Holy Cross College choir sang the Gospel of the Passion of Christ on Good Friday. Nothing of the vast liturgical reform we have since gone through could ever hope to capture the plaintive beauty of the Good Friday Reproaches, 'my people what have I done to you? How have I offended you? Answer me.' Nor has anyone been able to voice the sheer joy of the 'Exultet' hymn as Father Gozano did on Holy Saturday night. One unaccompanied voice soaring through the notes of the ancient hymn in the stillness of the packed cathedral had an immediate spiritual and emotional impact on me.

I began to wonder if it was possible to have a purely spiritual relationship with a priest. Biographies of saints always spoke of their 'spiritual director' – priests to whom the saint wrote or spoke for advice on matters of the soul. St Francis de Sales and St Jane Frances de Chantal were well known in the eighteenth century for the warm, loving and spiritual letters they wrote to each other and they'd both become saints. I thought I'd approach Father Stone. I liked the directness of his sermons and his humour. I bumped into him one morning as he was leaving the sacristy – that in itself had taken some organisation. 'Father, I wonder,' I said, summoning all my courage, 'would you consider becoming my spiritual director?' He looked as if I'd suggested we should jump off the cliffs at Tunnel Beach together. He moved sideways and stammered very quickly, 'Oh, Sister, that's a specialist's job – I think you ought to ask a specialist.' His was the quickest getaway I've seen anyone make.

Our confessor, though, was always a Dominican Father

*Science class at St Dominic's, 1925. My mother Min, back of front row, with long hair.*

*Min with Judith, her firstborn.*

Family group with car, 1938.

First Communion.

Standards 1, 2, 3, 4, St Joseph's, Papanui. Judith second from right, third row back.

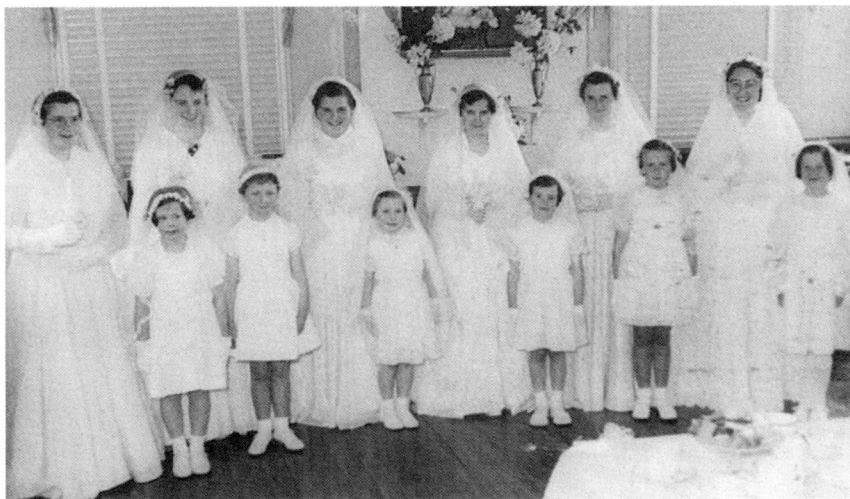

*Brides of Christ, October 1955. Judith with Marian as flowergirl, on end at right.*

*'Death to Self'. Final Vows Ceremony, January 1960.*

*Chanting the Divine Office in St Dominic's Chapel.*

*St Catherine's Girls Sports Day, c. 1966.*

from the North East Valley Priory and Aquinas Hall, now Aquinas College university hostel. Every Thursday afternoon at four a Dominican Father would hear the Sisters' confessions in the chapel sacristy. The secular mind marvels at what nuns could possibly have committed as sin in one week. Once I was kneeling behind Sister Benedict, a lovely old lay Sister, who suddenly panicked before her turn to go into the sacristy. At eighty years of age she was stuck with no obvious sin to confess. In a low voice she turned to me and said, 'What will I say? I can tell him I've been reading the *Woman's Weekly*.' (The height of decadence indeed.)

But the role of confessor was not just to hear our sins and grant forgiveness in God's name, but also to give positive spiritual direction. One of the confessors had an enormous influence on me, one T. P. Fitzgerald. He must have been about forty when he was made Prior at Aquinas Hall and he quickly became a favourite preacher, giving retreats, preaching the Sunday afternoon sermons, hearing our confessions and giving spiritual direction to many of the Sisters. He was a small, energetic man with a tremendous sense of the satirical and a great skill in communicating. He was positive and dominant and I thought he was marvellous. Many times in sessions of private spiritual direction I discussed my dissatisfaction with myself as a nun and my doubts about persevering. In reality, I was looking for attention from a man I admired. He kept talking about my introspection and my pride. I was not to be constantly comparing myself with others; I was to fix my attention on God and concentrate on doing what I should be doing, when I should be doing it and how I should be doing it. He felt I would make it.

The doubts certainly continued. One of my mother's favourite expressions had been, 'Don't tell me that you love me – prove it by what you do.' I had come to believe that the only way I could show God I loved Him was by staying on as a nun. But, in contrast to the peace of mind I had expected were I doing His will, I found myself constantly ill at ease and restless. I felt different from the others who seemed so unconsciously sure in their commitment. There were lighter moments. I was once kneeling in the nuns' transept at St Joseph's Cathedral behind the black iron grille. We were taking turns at silent prayer in a Parish Day of Recollection and I was on at the last hour from about 8.30pm. I was tossing my usual question to myself in distracted prayer, 'I don't want to be here, Lord, but if this is what you want for me I'll try – is it really what you want, Lord?' Suddenly Bishop Kavanagh came over to the grille. 'How long are you staying, Sister?' he asked. I was smitten with guilt. How could he know what I was thinking? I blushed furiously before I realised that all he wanted to know was when to lock up the church. And there was no one I could share that joke with later. Mother David, the Prioress General, had listened to my several requests to leave the Order. She always told me I would never be happy 'in the world' knowing I had not done what God expected me to do. Then she would send me away for a holiday, often with Sister Elizabeth and the late Sister Marie Grignon who were at university with me, to the convent in Queenstown or Teschemakers.

The Queenstown convent occupies a superb spot overlooking Lake Wakatipu, a two-storeyed stone building with a school attached at the back. In the early days there was a wooden two-storeyed building behind the convent and those Sisters who had tuberculosis were nursed back to health in the bracing alpine climate. But it was cold. The floors were wooden, the walls stone and there was little in the way of heating. The three or four of us lucky enough to be sent there on holiday still contrived to have a marvellous time. We were allowed to walk up Queenstown Hill for exercise and often the O'Connells who ran the hotel near the wharf sent up large grocery hampers of tinned foods and fresh fruit and dressed poultry so that we returned to Dunedin in great shape. I still love Queenstown and have a secret fascination for Moke Lake where we were taken by a kindly parishioner for an outing. I felt as though I were in some remote planet – the reflections in the lake, the stillness, the huge bare mountains and the green valley.

In 1959 I asked to be admitted to Final Profession, taking vows until death. This was the most solemn ceremony of all and certainly the most dramatic. The Sisters took their final vows publicly in front of their families and friends in the convent chapel. We were dressed in the full habit – that is, wearing the black cloak or 'cappa'. We promised commitment to Christ, kneeling at the feet of Mother Prioress General and then prostrated ourselves face down on the ground, covered by the black cappa and black veil. This was an obvious symbol of our 'death to self'.

To our parents it was a deeply painful moment – the final cut-off from the family. We had to be dead to the world in order to be alive in Christ.

This time I felt no elation of spirit at all – just a numb resolve to do what I did not want to do, but believed was what God wanted of me.

That year, too, I completed my B.A. Mother Catherine Laboure, the kindest of women and Mother Prioress at that time, came into the chapel one day in December with the university results. We were chanting Vespers and she sidled up beside me and passed me a card. All I saw was English III – 'A'. I was overjoyed. I had gained an 'A' the previous year for English II but this was the crowning touch. I felt I had finished university with a flourish. I would have been put to full-time teaching immediately the following year as we were very short of teaching Sisters in secondary, but I was called down to Dr Basil Howard's office – he was the university Liaison Officer – and told I had been awarded the Walter Scott Scholarship. I could study for my Master's if Mother Prioress General and her Council allowed me. I was very excited and very grateful when they did.

# CHAPTER 11

# CAMERON HOUSE

NINETEEN sixty-one was a memorable year. I was full time at university doing an M.A. in English. There were seven graduates that year and we had a marvellous time. The professors and lecturers who seemed so fearsome or remote suddenly became friends. I was given permission to attend morning tea with the staff and graduates on Fridays, although I was not allowed to eat or drink with them. For some inexplicable reason eating with lay people was thought of as inappropriate and worldly, although Christ had been recognised by his followers in the 'breaking of the bread'. This rule caused me great embarrassment. It seemed unreasonable and unnecessarily ill mannered to refuse those offering food and drink so generously.

A year before I had been sent to Christchurch with three other Sisters to go to a post-primary teachers' refresher course in History. It was held at Rangiora High School. I was amazed that the Council allowed me to go. It was my first visit home since I had entered about five years before. I couldn't stay at home of course but I was billeted with the other Sisters at the Sacred Heart convent in Ferry Road. My parents offered to drive us back and forth to Rangiora every day – quite an effort for them. On the Wednesday we had a free day and my mother asked the Sister in charge if we would all like to go to Akaroa for a picnic. The offer was readily accepted and my parents drove up to collect us with a full hamper of delicious food in the boot. When it was time for lunch, we found a very pretty spot near a waterfall up Aylmer's Valley Road, and my mother laid out all the food. Suddenly the senior Sister said, 'Mrs Hobbs, you realise that you and Mr Hobbs will be unable to eat with us ...' and my embarrassed parents took a plateful of food and disappeared around a corner. I was really angry at such an ungracious way of treating hospitality which had been given so generously. But I could do nothing. It was a rule, and we paid a great deal of reverence to rules rather than people in those days. A nun sacrificed much to serve Christ, but often her family sacrificed even more. I was about to accompany Mother David to the Milton convent one weekend in 1961 when a Sister asked her if she could travel to be with her dying father in Invercargill. She had been allowed to visit him in hospital shortly before, but now, on his deathbed, he was calling out loud for his favourite daughter. I froze as Mother David said firmly, 'Sister, you cannot go again. You have already had the privilege of seeing him in hospital. And you know the Rule forbids us to visit our family homes.' I felt sick standing there and watching the Sister's anguish. She did not see her father alive again.

But at university in 1961, I quickly – perhaps too quickly

and easily – became part of a family. Professor Horsman, Dr Margaret Dalziel, Gregor Cameron, Lenore Harty, Bob Robertson, Colin Gibson and Keith Maslen led us in hilarious or serious discussions over Milton and Jane Austen and Beowulf, Chaucer and King Lear. I was stimulated mentally in a way I had never known. Every day was exciting. My close friend that year was Jocelyn Wood (Harris) now Associate Professor of English at Otago. She had a slow, relaxed manner of talking which put you immediately at ease and belied the razor-sharp logic of the mind behind it. We had to give a seminar to the staff on Milton and while I dutifully prepared a scholastic note on Pastoralism and 'Lycidas', Jocelyn took an entirely novel approach to Milton's 'Paradise Lost' and defended it with great courage and skill. Dr Dalziel had prepared us for it and her advice to me was, 'Don't gabble, Sister'. She told Jocelyn, 'You're very brave. You'll be shot down in flames'.

Those remarks probably indicated the difference between Jocelyn and me. I was a student. Jocelyn was more. She was an original thinker. In exams I would write furiously and every time I looked up Jocelyn would be staring out the window. She was thinking. I was remembering. At the end of that year Jocelyn got married and asked Mother Prioress if she could see me at St Dominic's on the way to the church. I was immensely touched that she would come out of her way on such a day.

Cameron House, sadly, has gone. It was such a gracious wooden building full of beautifully shaped rooms, each reflecting its lecturer's taste and personality. We looked out magic casements on to a green lawn and lovely trees. It was a Brideshead year. Before the last lecture we were photographed as a very happy group out on the front lawn.

In 1961 I spent most of my days outside my school classes at the university, being allowed now to study in the library. My lecture in Anglo-Saxon was at eleven in the morning and I was in a class of one. I tried desperately to keep awake while dear Mr Cameron explained the intricacies of 'Beowulf' but in the end I did the unpardonable. I didn't go to any more lectures from about July and worked instead in the stackroom of the library. About a month before the exams I bumped into Mr Cameron in the quad. I blushed in confusion and he said so kindly, 'Oh, Sister, you must have been ill – I know – you don't need to tell me. What about answering some questions for me for revision?' I felt a heel, collected the work and did some essays and notes perfunctorily. Back they came, marked and annotated, with four pages of additional notes all in his own handwriting. I looked at them cursorily, put them at the back of my bookshelf, and promptly forgot them. In his exam I read the questions, blinked, read again – they were the very ones he had asked me to do a month earlier. I sat numb at my desk with tears spilling on to the paper – I couldn't remember a thing. It was just deserts.

When the university year ended with the last exams in November 1961 I felt utterly dejected. I realised how much I had enjoyed the liberation of thought that my M.A. year had given me, and the exciting life outside the convent walls.

I was also teaching senior classes in English and History and now I threw myself into pre-exam revison for them. The Mistress of Schools (the principal) was very aware the school's reputation in the eyes of the community rested on examination results, public speaking awards, sporting triumphs as well as the high standard of student behaviour. It was a source of great pride therefore when Jocelyn Trewby won a University Scholarship and when the public speaking team from St Dominic's won the Bishop's Shield. We also entered girls for the Anthony Eden Speech Contest and I was deputed to 'help', that is, write the speeches. I enjoyed this because I was aware of the power a gifted public speaker can have over an audience. We won several of these contests.

My youngest sister, Marian, was now at St Dominic's. She had begged to come boarding in form one and my parents had given in to her. She seemed to thrive at school, even when I was her History teacher. Pupils could not tell our voices apart and she created much stir if she called out to someone down a corridor and the person couldn't see which one of us it was. Even now when she talks on radio I get comments on all sorts of ideas I am supposed to have given voice to.

By the end of that November I was physically very tired. I could talk to no one about how much I missed university; didn't it just sound like intellectual arrogance? About this time we were told that Pat, one of our six, had left the Order from a suburban convent and returned to secular life. We all felt as if someone had died. There was a brief, impersonal announcement and the novitiate was bathed in sadness. She was never mentioned again – it was as if she had gone to another planet. We received a bright and breezy letter from her some months later about her new job and friends but there was an unspoken belief among us that she wasn't as happy as she sounded – how could she be?

There were amazing stories we picked up in convent gossip of what had happened to those unfortunate Sisters who had forsaken their vows and left. I knew none of these Sisters but felt I knew them all. One had married an alcoholic and suffered terribly, another had become mentally ill. The general theme was unhappiness. A refusal to accept God's offer meant you would always be unhappy. The Sister who left, left with the stigma of failure and she would feel guilty forever. It was as if the Church could never admit that people made mistakes. Lifelong commitments, made when you were twenty, were forever and there was no going back. I wish there had been stories of a nun leaving defiantly, shouting abuse and storming out banging the cloister door. But rigid self-control was the hallmark of every Sister and nothing like this ever happened. The Catholic community was not usually welcoming to lapsed nuns or priests. They were spoken of in whispers. When an Irish Sister left from our novitiate and chose to stay in New Zealand she kept writing to her parents in Ireland for at least a year as if she was still a nun. She was happily working in an office here but there was no way she could tell her parents of the awful truth. So with all my doubts and depression I kept silent. Just to talk about it to another Sister would have provoked horror.

I did talk to Mother David, the Prioress General. She seemed to take a personal interest in my case and would make exceptions for me. She was always welcoming and kind to me, although she could be stern with others, and I was able to go to her directly, bypassing the senior Sisters. But the various Mother Prioresses who worked under her were more conventional – I was not to be treated differently from any other Sister.

That November in 1961 I felt the coldness, sterility and claustrophobia of convent life unbearable after the warmth and friendliness of Cameron House. Then I was called to Mother Prioress's office for a reprimand. I was becoming too friendly, too casual in my behaviour with my pupils. I was forgetting my status as a nun – a person apart. But it was even more specific. 'After school last Friday while you were cleaning windows with the monitors you were heard laughing and talking immoderately, Sister, and – I can't believe this – one of the senior girls saw you smoking.' I was stunned, not so much by the hilarious picture of a nun with a cigarette hanging out of her mouth cleaning corridor windows, but that such a rumour could be entertained, that the Mother Prioress actually believed that it could happen. Of course it wasn't true. But I was too worldly in her eyes. I was not behaving as a religious Sister should. I took my reprimand with my eyes lowered as I had been trained but I was fuming and upset. All Saturday I was in a turmoil. This was the end. I had to get out. I'd said I wasn't good enough over and over again. Why hadn't I been allowed to go earlier? If they didn't trust me there was little point in staying. I was more bitter than I'd ever felt before. I had to – run away?

To leave the Order legitimately once a Sister was professed required a formal application to a religious tribunal in Rome. The letter had to go through the correct channels and it could take at least two months. That day I wasn't interested in anything except getting out fast. I did not wish to go through complicated formalities or be told any more of God's special love for me.

I couldn't run away wearing a habit. I had somehow to find some 'civvies' that fitted. The boarders were out on Sundays and I sped round to Marian's dormitory and rustled through her wardrobe. My hair was cropped very short – I had to have a scarf or something to tie around it. I was feverish with determination and fear. I disappeared into a school toilet in the Rosary Hall basement and changed. There was no mirror so I couldn't see how odd I looked. I just headed out the gate behind the cathedral sacristy and down into the anonymity of Rattray Street, my eyes blinded with tears. I knew I couldn't keep walking the streets. The only outside person I felt I could trust was my university tutor, Margaret Dalziel. I phoned her from a telephone box, using pennies I had found in Marian's locker.

# CHAPTER 12

# REPERCUSSIONS

MARGARET Dalziel was and still is a formidable lady but I instinctively turned to her for help that day and I am not at all surprised that I did so. I loved her as a lecturer and respected her immensely as a friend. She does not show affection easily but that day I knew the depths of her kindness. She didn't sound a bit surprised or shocked – and she must have been. One does not expect such a phone call at lunch on a Sunday. She told me she had no car, but I could get to Opoho by bus, and there I went. People were staring at me. Perhaps I looked like a battered wife – I was crying quietly and looking away from the bus passengers and out the window. I found her house and I can't remember anything of those few hours except that she listened and listened while cooking me a lovely meal. I could eat only half of it. She is a lady of great religious faith herself and perhaps that is why I went to her. I did not want to talk to someone who would find religious life incomprehensible and laughable. It wasn't a joke – I was in a crisis; I was in the wrong place and again I wanted someone to make a decision for me – a decision I felt too scared or too guilty to make myself. How could one turn God down?

At some stage she said, 'Oughtn't I let somebody know?' and after some thought I told her to ring my spiritual director, Father T. P. Fitzgerald, at Aquinas Hall. It was another example of how quickly I shelved the personal responsibility for the direction of my life. He would tell me I should leave. He didn't. He was, I gather, fairly brusque with Margaret and said he was sending round a car for me and I was to go there. I remember Margaret saying, 'Don't let them talk you into going back if you don't want to.' And I smiled wanly at her. How I wished I had been a Protestant. Mind you, John Knox and Calvin might have been just as good at stirring up guilt.

Brother Martin collected me at half-past two and I was whisked up to Aquinas Hall. Father Fitzgerald was very kind and talked of the stress of study, my habit of judging myself alongside others, my general dispiritedness. He was kind and warm and funny and somehow by six o'clock I was back at St Dominic's being put to bed by the Sister Infirmarian and visited by Mother Prioress and Mother Prioress General who spoke to me in soothing whispers and treated me as if I had had a severe emotional breakdown. No one else was told anything of it. No one else knew. Marian's clothes were returned before she had even missed them. I was told to sleep in for the next three mornings – the exam strain had been, the Infirmarian said, too much for me. I was cosseted for the next month, taken off duties, sent away on trips with Mother David until I seemed back to normal.

Then the results came out and I got my masters with

second class honours. I was bitterly disappointed. I had hoped for first class and thought I might just have made it in spite of my fated Old English paper. But I knew in my heart that I wasn't a first class academic. And there was another reason. I was being punished. God was not to be mocked, and I had made a mockery of my commitment to Him. I had shamed the Order by talking to an outsider. I felt I was justly punished. I was proud and had put human values ahead of spiritual ones. In the refectory a week before I had had to do Cross Prayers publicly – I stood in front of other Sisters at the table and extended my arms in the form of a cross while silently reciting the psalm *Miserere*, King David's lament that Christ had quoted on the cross. It is the penance for serious breaches of the Rule. As I said the cross prayers I felt truly dead myself. I didn't deserve love from anyone, much less God. No one knew that was the penance I was given for running away. And that was light. The Constitution laid down punishments like fasting on bread and water – but Father Fitzgerald must have put in a plea for clemency.

# CHAPTER 13

# MOTHER SEBASTIAN

IT took a long time before I felt at all settled again, but I threw myself into teaching and it helped. I stayed at St Dominic's for the following two years. I knew that Jocelyn and the others in my Honours year would be back in Dunedin to be capped in May, but no Dominican Sisters were allowed to be capped. I imagine this was to prevent our becoming proud. I didn't see or hear from any of them. I was cut off from my university friends, which is what I should have expected.

More girls won scholarships, among them Sandra Winton, possibly the most gifted student I had ever taught. She was a generous, open-natured pupil and extremely sensitive. She entered the Order a few months before I left. Then there were Bernadette and Elizabeth, both excellent writers, who gained Lissie Rathbone Prizes and went on to do law (Elizabeth) or become a published poet (Bernadette). There was Denise, loyal and reliable, and the Enright twins who spent their lives trying to confuse me. And there were many others.

But there were other jobs to be done around the convent

apart from teaching. I put myself in charge of getting rid of burnable rubbish. Behind the cathedral sacristy were several old drums used by the nuns to burn old textbooks, papers, exercises – any rubbish around. I spent many hours at the burner. My friends began calling it 'Steve's burning passion'. I also had weekly duties along with the other junior professed Sisters in the vast kitchen of the ground floor of the Priory. Sister Paul was the cook then for about 56 nuns and 55 boarders. It was a demanding and physically exhausting job. The nuns' refectory was on the first floor and at dinner time, 12.30pm, I would help her stack lidded plates one at a time in rows on the shelves of the dumb waiter which we then pulled up by rope to the slide in the dining room. The plates had to be carefully stacked so that a slight jolt would not cause them all to come tumbling down the chute, covering us in hot stew and mashed potatoes. There was a precise moment between the singing of Grace upstairs and the beginning of the Reading when we had to pull the slide up. The boarders were fed in the room adjoining the kitchen at the same time so we were rushing round, prayerfully of course, for about fifteen minutes.

Sister Paul and I got on very well together. We should have – Paul and Stephen were responsible for each other's canonisation in the early Church. Sister Paul was a fabulous cook. She knew somehow I had been in trouble. She would never talk about it but there was a compassion there I was very aware of. She teased me mercilessly. I was much slower at getting the plates stacked than she was and she'd often call out, 'Come on, Lightning – get moving.'

But the most valuable experience I had at St Dominic's was when I was assigned to help in the infirmary. It provided a great insight into the human heart.

When a Sister grew too old for active work or for following the daily routine of the convent she was looked after in the infirmary. I have never seen such love and care bestowed on any other human as I saw daily in the infirmary. The Sisters in charge of the sick were Sisters Fabian and Alban in my day. The infirmary was on the sunny side of the main Priory building above the nun's parlour. There was a kitchenette, a bathroom, an enormous toilet raised up like a throne and a little sunroom overlooking the harbour and the city. There were individual cells going off the corridor for those Sisters still able to move around and there were two sick rooms for those who were bedridden. Here I was privileged to look after Sister Lucy, Mother Frigidian, Sister Dominic and Mother Sebastian.

Sister Lucy was the sweetest old lady of them all. She had been a very hard-working lay Sister and was much loved by Sisters Fabian and Alban, lay Sisters themselves. She spent her time sewing or reading or stumbling up to the chapel gallery to pray – she prayed for us all all day – I never heard her moan or complain about anyone or anything. In spite of her stiffening joints she grew more content as she grew older.

Mother Frigidian (totally misnamed, but after an Irish Saint) was a very handsome woman with blazing black eyes and marble skin. I also admired her forthrightness. Once when I told her I often thought of giving up, her usually gentle face froze and she looked at me sternly and said, 'Go down on your knees, Sister, and ask God for forgiveness'. I learnt to be more discreet, in view of her heart condition.

Sister Dominic was in her nineties and had been an ascetic Mother Superior in her time. She was a woman of dignity and intelligence and was very aware of her upper class background. She was the religious version of Lady Bracknell. She had a deep and cultured voice and once when she was taking a visitor past the chapel she came upon the two Murphy girls, Gwynne and Noreen, who were cleaning the brass. They were splendid girls, both blessed with a marvellous sense of humour and were unusually tall. Mother Dominic glanced at them, nodded and said in a stage whisper to the visitor, 'They're the Murphy girls. People say they are very nice, but they're too tall'. Mother Dominic went quietly senile and was convinced until her death that there were *men* in her room, in the wardrobe, under the bed. We junior Sisters had to go along with this charade before we could get her to go to sleep and many's the imaginary Tom or John I furiously chased out of her room.

My favourite of all in the infirmary was Mother Sebastian. She was a little dumpling of a nun and had been a wonderful mathematics teacher. She had also been a Bursar in charge of the finances of the convent. Her mind had gone too and all the honest but critical thoughts she'd kept to herself all those years came tumbling out. I can't remember all the stories about Mother Sebastian in her old age when I knew her, but there are some...

She was quite strong physically and often went wandering all over the convent. This would have been fine, but she never quite finished dressing herself and she embarrassed the life out of many a young curate by walking in on him dressed only in her singlet and long knickers while he was having breakfast after mass. 'Are they looking after you, Father?' she would ask ever so kindly, oblivious to the shock on his face. Sister Alban would come quickly in and try to lead her away but if she wanted to have a conversation with Father, she would have a conversation. She loved the convent cat, a huge black panther called Jojo, who led a blessed existence. If a Sister wanted another Sister in the convent she would call her by ringing the handbell a certain number of times. I was number forty – that required four peels. Thirty-six was three peels and six strokes. Mother Prioress General was one stroke and whenever Mother Sebastian heard that, she would call, 'Jojo, you're wanted downstairs'.

One day she wandered a little too far in her underwear, right down Rattray Street in fact. No one knew how she got out in the first place, but how would we get her back? She ignored the girls sent out specially and urgently; 'Be discreet, but hurry'. In the end as the little figure stumbled on doggedly, heading towards Speight's brewery, Bishop Kavanagh was called on. Now he was a very shy man and this must have been a peculiarly onerous pastoral duty. He failed totally. She brushed him aside, even when he showed her his purple armband. 'I am your Bishop, and I am ordering you to return to your convent.' She would have none of it. 'Young man, you have no jurisdiction over me.' And Mother Sebastian swept past him. In the end Sister Alban was given permission to go outside the cloister in the convent car and rescue this wayward soul. I think she told her dinner was served and in that way Mother Sebastian was restored to the fold – and the decencies of the habit.

She did not like the old lay Sister, Sister Benedict, one bit. For years Mother Sebastian must have controlled all her feelings but now she really picked on Sister Benedict. She scathingly remarked on Sister Benedict's lack of personal hygiene, her messiness at table and her general clumsiness. Sister Benedict knew there was nothing for it but to avoid Mother Sebastian and eventually she had the good sense to die. The coffin of every dead Sister lay open in state in the chapel while the Office of the Dead and Penitential Psalms were said. Sister Gregory and I were taking our turn praying on either side of the coffin in the chapel when we heard the distinctive shuffle of Mother Sebastian. We braced ourselves. Mother Sebastian wove towards the coffin and took a long look at her innocent enemy lying so still. 'You're not looking yourself at all today, Sister,' she said quite wistfully to the corpse.

She knew the Divine Office psalms off by heart and we used to get convulsions if we looked up and saw her holding her breviary upside down, the pages marked not by holy pictures but by thin wedges of toilet paper. Once in choir I saw her trying to balance a big safety pin on her nose as if it were spectacles. Towards the end she was confined to bed and then there were no more wanderings. I took her in a cup of tea one night. She looked like a kewpie doll in bed. 'There's some biscuits coming in a minute,' I said. She turned to the wall, 'Tom,' she said, 'there's some biscuits coming.' I fled. I wasn't prepared to cope with yet more men. Mother Sebastian died very peacefully quite soon after this and I felt bereft. She had been such fun and it had been wonderful to see her puckish personality surfacing at the end in spite of all her training.

When the Sisters were dying they were never left alone and each of the community Sisters was given an hour's bedside duty. I was quite scared at first especially if my time was three to four in the morning. The Infirmarian was always on call and we knew to watch for any change in breathing patterns. Sometimes the dying Sister would hold my hand tightly and it struck me as odd that these women whose whole life was a preparation for death should let life go so reluctantly. Death was often a long, slow process but when the Infirmarian saw the change, all the Sisters would be called and we would kneel around the bed and sing the very plaintive and beautiful 'Salve Regina', a hymn we sang to Our Lady every night in Compline. I often wondered what effect this must have had on the dying Sister if it is true that the sense of hearing is the last to go. Would she know that this was her last moment? It was always the most solemn occasion to me as a young nun, the most telling reminder of my own mortality. When a Sister died the Infirmarian and another Sister helped to lay the body out. The open coffin was taken to the chapel where the Sister lay in state for about a day. After all the prayers for the dead had been said, the coffin would be carried down the steep stone steps at the end of the glass cloister while the community formed a guard of honour and sang the 'Salve Regina' again. It was the Order's formal goodbye to one of its members. The Bishop or a senior priest would then say a Requiem Mass in the cathedral and the coffin would be taken by the undertaker privately to, I think, the southern cemetery.

Most Sisters died of old age or heart attacks. Sudden death, even in the convent, was always a shock. If a Sister had been dying for some time the death bell indicated her happy release, but the sudden tolling of the bell in the middle of the day stopped everyone in their tracks. Sister Bernadine died right after having breakfast in bed – she had been ill for two days – and I remember everyone being impressed that she had pushed the tray away before she died so there was no mess. Another Sister died in the toilet at Dominican Hall. Four Sisters were killed in one road accident in Southland. So convents were not spared the tragedy of the human condition. There was even a saying that nuns died in threes, especially in November, the month devoted to prayers for the dead. And when we weren't too busy, we would wonder morbidly who would be next.

There was humour though. I once asked Sister Zedislava in North East Valley about the condition of a Sister who had been ill. She answered, 'Mortification has set in'. My glasses broke just after Mother Xavier had died and Mother Prioress suggested I wear the glasses she had left behind. Mercifully I managed to persuade her that I still wouldn't be able to see and my own glasses were fixed. I wondered what would have happened if I'd had false teeth and broken them. Recycling was a convent custom long before it was popular with environmentalists.

# CHAPTER 14

# THE ORDER OF THE DAY

A Dominican Sister's day began at 5.30am, unless we were on refectory or infirmary duty when we were up at five. We dressed speedily without mirrors and tried to be down in the chapel by 5.50 so that we could do the Stations of the Cross before 6am when the morning Hours of the Divine Office were chanted. We stood in two rows facing each other and chanted alternate verses of the psalms. If we were praying privately we knelt in our stall facing the altar. At 6.30 we sat in silence to meditate on a passage from a spiritual book we had read. As professed Sisters we were allowed to choose our spiritual reading. At 6.55 one of the parish priests would arrive to say mass for the community. This would be over by 7.40 when we would all process down through the glass cloister to the refectory for breakfast, chanting the hymn of thanksgiving, 'Te Deum Laudamus'.

Breakfast was a quick affair of porridge or stewed prunes or figs, toast and tea. While we were being served by the refectorians one of the novices would read aloud a chapter from *The Imitation of Christ* by Thomas A'Kempis. After that we would move back to the chapel for brief private prayers and then go upstairs to make our beds and leave our cells 'in perfect order and neatness'. By 8.20 most of us would have finished our house duties and would be taking a twenty minute music or speech lesson.

Morning school went from 9am till 12.20pm. We had a quick morning interval for a cup of tea unless we were on duty. The main meal of the day was served at 12.30. Unlike tea, it was of two substantial courses and if the Sister in charge of the kitchen was a superb cook, and most were, it was also very satisfying. We had corned beef, stews, fish on Wednesdays and Fridays, shepherd's pie, all served with three vegetables. On Sundays and first class feasts there was always a roast. Sunday breakfast included oranges and honey. Those were very special days.

At midday dinner we would again be read to by the Reader Sister from the Gospel, the Constitutions of the Order and then from an entertaining secular book. On Fridays, as if to emphasise the penitential character of the day, the Sister read the entire Rule of St Augustine. This, while eating steamed fish and boiled rice, made it a particularly awful day. But it was very pleasant being read to at meals and we didn't get indigestion from talking and eating at once. The secular books we heard were always interesting – adventure stories, travel books, autobiographies like *I, George Nepia* (we had some great rugby fans in the convent hierarchy). No fiction was read. I was a reader for several years and loved the job although it was ghastly for both me and the Sisters eating if I had a cold and blocked nose.

After lunch those Sisters who were free were able to have about twenty minutes of recreation, usually sitting in the sun of the long glass cloister or walking up and down outside in the convent garden. It was a pity no one could see over the fence into this pretty, sheltered garden as the sight of two long lines of nuns walking back and forth talking to each other would have enchanted the paparrazzi. Walking backwards in those long habits while talking nineteen to the dozen was quite a skill and yet I don't remember anyone ever tripping.

At 1.30 we were back at school again till 3.30 when we supervised the cleaning of the classrooms we had used. Mostly this involved sweeping the floors with damp tea leaves and dusting and straightening the desks with the class monitors. The toilets were also scrupulously cleaned and on Friday all the classroom floors were polished. Once a month we cleaned every window using wet and dry newspapers. Some of us then taught music or speech to private pupils until 5pm when the chapel bell went for Vespers. At 5.30 began another half hour of walking recreation, and tea followed at 6pm – baked beans on toast or sausages in gravy, watery tomatoes and onions or a very glutinous form of macaroni cheese. Again we were read to. At 6.30 we were back in the chapel for Matins (for the next day's feast) and the evening's private meditation. We might then have twenty minutes for class preparation or study and of course some of us were on duty with the boarders. At 8pm we gathered for an hour of recreation in the community room. This was the most relaxing period of the day when we sat and talked and laughed, mended our clothes or embroidered innumerable tray cloths.

At 9pm the Profound Silence bell would ring and we would return to the chapel for night prayers and the beautiful chant of Compline. We could then study for another twenty minutes in our own cells but, unless we had special permission, the lights were out at 10pm. It was a long and very busy day, a day without any space. The weekends were not much different. We 'slept in' until 6am on Saturdays and 6.30am on Sundays. Most of Saturday morning was spent in a thorough cleaning of various parts of the convent and after the midday meal we usually had a free afternoon for study or class preparation. Some Saturday nights, especially if it were a feast day, we would watch a film borrowed from the National Library. Our favourites were always thrillers or murder mysteries. But often on a Saturday night an ex-pupil or parishioner recently returned from overseas would show us slides of her trip. I think we knew Lourdes and Rome better than most of their citizens.

Sunday was a slower day, masses in the morning, class preparation in the afternoon. On the first Sunday of every month we had a day of total silence and recollection, usually with a special sermon given in the chapel in mid-afternoon. Many Sisters went to three masses in the morning that day; the chapel mass and the two parish masses in the cathedral. I always had a tussle with my conscience as to whether I attend the 11am mass or do some much needed study. In the afternoon we often had a choir practice if a feast day mass and office were coming up in the week ahead. On fourth Sunday afternoons we were allowed to see visitors for two hours and could serve them afternoon tea in the visitors' parlour.

There were special days of celebration in the convent as when Sisters were professed or had reached an anniversary of profession, silver or golden. The morning of the celebration we set up long tables in the glass cloister with afternoon tea for visiting Sisters and the families of the celebrants. Spotless white linen tablecloths were brought up from the pantries on the ground floor along with the tiered plates of prepared sandwiches and butterfly cakes and the polished silver service. In the middle of all was the enormous iced anniversary cake. Once in the middle of such an afternoon tea Mother Philomena hushed us all. 'I have asked one of our guests for a special favour. Miss Mina Foley is going to sing for us.' From one side of the cloister the crowds parted and revealed a shy dark girl who began singing an unaccompanied aria. It was spell-binding. I have never heard so exquisite a sound. Then just as suddenly she stopped, mid-song, and there was only the slightest embarrassed pause as she turned back into the crowd before we burst out clapping. (We were told later to our sadness that the staggering potential of her singing career had been cut short by serious illness.) I wish we had heard more.

Nuns were not often ill. 'Your health is our responsibility, but you owe it to the Order to keep well,' Mother Tarcisius had taught us. So we were well looked after if we were genuinely ill. Our life was so regular that all we seemed to get were the common classroom colds and flu. But the stress of the daily routine also meant that laxatives were a frequent medicine. If our illness was beyond the scope of the Infirmarian the convent doctor would be sent for. In most cases he was a devout Catholic – that was far more important than his medical expertise. I remember only one doctor whom the nuns called on who was not a Catholic and that was Dr Stubbs in Oamaru. He and his son were both no-nonsense men and very good diagnosticians. Their surgery was part of their large, rambling house and we frequently met several of the numerous brood of very uninhibited children who tumbled in and out of rooms very much like Dickens's Pocket family. It was a tonic in itself to visit them.

# CHAPTER 15

# HOLIDAYS

ONCE the boarders had left a great quiet spread over vast areas of St Dominic's. 'Sister Stephen, would you and Sister Denise be in charge of the girls' dormitories? They are to be thoroughly cleaned and aired.' The end of the school year was the signal for a massive tidy-up of places that most people would consider tidy anyway. We dusted and polished, scrubbed and disinfected dormitories, bathrooms and the dining hall and then we closed them up unless visiting Sisters from other convents came in for retreats. For the first week or so of the holidays I missed the liveliness of the pupils and was thrown upon my own meagre resources. These feelings of inadequacy became more acute as in May and before Christmas we would go into retreat. These were periods of either three or nine days of total silence on our part and spiritual direction from the Retreat Master given either privately or in sermons in the chapel. We had about three sermons a day. The Sisters would come in to the main convents from the outlying convents like Cromwell, Queenstown, Lawrence, Milton, North East Valley and Kaikorai. And we would all make places for them, shifting to accommodate their superior rank in both chapel and refectory, and giving them our cells while we moved to the boarding school dormitories – I always resented that. Mother David took the view that the nuns in the bigger convents should also have a change and we would be sent by bus to Teschemakers or Invercargill to make our retreats there. Teschemakers was, and is, a beautiful place set in a treed valley inland from Oamaru. The grounds and property had been gifted to the Order by Mother Philomena's relatives, the McCarthy family. It was a rather splendid boarding school in its day for the moneyed Catholics of Canterbury and North Otago. Its lovely grounds, swimming pool and surrounding countryside were a favourite holiday destination for the Sisters. There is a very impressive chapel, one of the few consecrated Catholic chapels in the South Island. It was an inspiring place to make a retreat and I loved the several summers I spent there.

The nine days' retreat before Christmas was a very beautiful preparation for the feast. I loved the liturgy and feast of Easter far more, but the ancient 'O' antiphons we sang daily in choir from the sixteenth of December were special. Christ, about to be born, is addressed in words that link both Hebrew and Christian imagery, and each antiphon begins with the vocative 'O' – O Wisdom, O Adonais, O Root of Jesse, O Key of David – and as the feast gets closer the sentiment becomes more intense. But the actual feast of Christmas was a time of sadness for me. It is so much a family feast that no amount of sublimation could make it half as good as it was at home. Of course, we received gifts from our family and Christmas cards and we were allowed visitors but I was always homesick that day. My own feast day, St Stephen's, was the day after Christmas and I know how cheated children born near Christmas Day feel. It was always the day after. Even if I had been truly committed to religious life I doubt that I would have ever appreciated a convent Christmas.

I blame my feelings on my mother. She worked at making Christmas memorable, even in the days of wartime rationing. We nearly always had a tree and when we were very small, I remember she made footprints in lollies from the chimney to the tree. On the table beside the tree there was always a glass of beer and a piece of fruit cake for the man who came down the chimney. The table would be beautifully decorated for the Christmas meal, even when we had very little money.

After Christmas at Teschemakers the younger Sisters did as much class preparation as we could for the coming year. We often had lectures from senior Sisters who were experienced teachers but these were mostly for Christian Doctrine lessons. During the 1960s a programme was set up to send each year two Sisters with obvious potential as spiritual leaders to study at one of the many theological colleges in Rome. Sisters Jordan and Genevieve were the first to go and I remember looking at them with awe as we said the Travellers' Prayers in chapel before they left. It seemed such a long way to go and such a long time to be away from New Zealand. The lectures they gave us when they returned were full of new insights into Church history and doctrine and they had wonderful stories of their experiences, the places they had seen, the people they had met. I knew it was pointless my wishing to be sent

*Emmet in his clericals at Greenmeadows.*

*Family group (without Gillian) at Teschemakers.*

English Honours group at University of Otago, 1961.
From left, Beverley Allott, Anne Paterson, Jocelyn Wood, Chris Duval-Smith, Judith.
In front, Pat Pacey, Stella Williams.

English lecturers 1961.
From left, Keith Maslen, Lenore Harty, Gregor Cameron,
Alan Horsman, Margaret Dalziel, Bob Robertson.

*Teaching at St Catherine's, Invercargill.*

*Invercargill visitors, Marian and Emmet.*

*Wedding Day,*
*20 December 1968.*

*Three generations. From left, Min with Kirsty at two months, Judith and Gill.*

though Sister Cecily often said, 'You'll be off, Steve. Just you wait. I bet you'll be sent next year'. But I knew I had blotted my copybook permanently and I wouldn't be trusted far from the Motherhouse.

Every January when all my friends met again for retreat and the holidays, they had great stories of community life in the smaller convents. It sounded more relaxed than life at the Motherhouse. We had long sessions down by the river on who were good Superiors and who were strict and what convents and schools were good to work in. We knew the Superiors who were sticklers for rules, the ones who worked their Sisters hard, the ones with senses of humour. Most of my group enjoyed their new and responsible life at places like the School for the Deaf at Feilding or the little convents in Lawrence, Milton, Queenstown and Cromwell. Bluff was highly favoured. 'You don't feel someone is watching you all the time,' Sister Mary said. 'You're always under the eyes of the councillors at St Dominic's.'

These four councillors were elected, with the Mother Prioress General, for three years, and could be re-elected for another three. It was a democratic process, each convent electing a delegate to represent them at the Chapter. They nominated and then voted for Sisters to be on the council. It was a very solemn occasion, done in committee in the chapel. The general criteria seemed to be that a nominated Sister had to be healthy, but not too healthy or she would not be compassionate to those who weren't as strong as she was; intelligent, but not too intelligent or she would not tolerate the limitations of those she worked with; and holy, but not too holy or she would not be aware of what was happening around her. The office of Mother Prioress General was a particularly onerous position and both Mother Philomena and Mother David in my time were re-elected and served for six long years. Mother Philomena was often seen attacking weeds in the garden early on summer mornings and we all knew it was her way of dealing with stress.

The councillors were the advisors to the Prioress General. They were all senior Sisters in age, kind and cautious, chosen for their wisdom and experience. Theoretically, if there was an obvious personality conflict in one of the smaller convents, a Sister could approach any of these councillors and negotiate a transfer, but in practice in my day they were solid supporters of the status quo and unanimously conservative. I didn't hear of any great unhappiness in these small convents other than that of the generation gap – one Sister aged twenty-two living with three others aged fifty-four, sixty-one and seventy-six. This could make living together a lonely experience for the junior. She was also expected to do a lot of the harder physical work in and around the classroom because she was younger.

I seemed permanently attached to St Dominic's. I had been made First Chantress responsible for the correct singing of the Divine Office, the choral preparation for feast days and the assigning of choral duties. It was a duty I thoroughly enjoyed. When Mother David tapped with her ring on her prie-dieu that was a signal for me to hit the note of G unaccompanied and begin the Office with the prayer '*Deus in adjutorium meum intende*'. If I went on to intone the wrong psalm or hymn a senior Sister would quickly cut in and correct me, so I had to prepare the Office thoroughly. Compline was the only accompanied plain chant – there was an organ in the chapel gallery. Mother David had decided that all the Sisters who could play the piano, with whatever ability, should take turns at accompanying the choir at Compline. I was petrified at having to accompany the others because I had to listen very carefully from upstairs and I never seemed to get either the right volume or the right pace. Once I pulled out all the wrong stops and started to blast the choir away and a Sister was sent up to replace me – my accompaniment was too awful for devotion. I was mortified.

Mother Patricia once told me that she thought she was too proud when she was a novice and prayed to be humiliated.

'I could never do that,' I said. 'I don't need to. Were your prayers answered?'

'They were indeed,' she said with a wry smile. 'It was my turn to answer mass and as I went to lift the handbell for the consecration [the most solemn part of mass] its handle came away in my hand and the whole three-toned bell fell to the ground and rolled to the corner with an enormous crash. Even the priest jumped. As I got up to get it as noiselessly as I could I tripped on the prie-dieu. Another Sister was motioned by the Prioress to take my place.'

We would swap these reminiscences at Teschemakers during picnics at Gemmell's Crossing while we waited for the billy to boil or on long walks down the paddocks in front of the convent to the river. For a week or so in those lovely summers we could relax. We could even swim in the school pool – but not lie around sunbathing afterwards. We were still nuns.

One glorious hot day Mother Borromeo announced that we were going to Moeraki Beach for a picnic. Huge hampers of sandwiches, piles of boiled eggs and lettuce leaves, slabs of fruit cake and bottles of cordial were packed and we all drove off to the beach. Some of us swam in the surf for the first time in many years and we walked along the beach. I don't know how it happened but there seemed very few other people there that hot sunny day and we had a small part of the Pacific to ourselves. Next morning during his breakfast the priest who said mass told Sister St Ann, 'I've never seen such raw and blistered faces peering from habits in my life'. It was a day we all talked about for months.

In mid-January the relaxed holiday air around the place began to give way to nervous tension. The bulls were coming. These were the typed assignation notices given to the Sisters who were going to be moved from one convent to the other. They were placed on the Sister's seat in the chapel. Sometimes they were promotion notices. A Sister would open her bull and find that she was now the Superior of the Sisters listed below in a small community in, say, Queenstown. There were enormous talking sessions about who would go where before the bulls came out, and near the day, large cut-out animal bulls would appear on various noticeboards. (The word bull came, of course, from papal bulls, edicts from the Pope with his seal affixed.) We used to rehearse the worst possible scenarios. 'I couldn't cope if she became my Superior.' 'Holy St Anthony, you don't think I'll be sent to Santa Sabina, do you?'

And then one evening we would go to the chapel and in silence open our bull. I never had one. I used to come out afterwards and listen spellbound to the excitement around me. 'She's too young to be a Superior. What are they thinking of?' 'Oh God help us, Steve, I've got to be cook at Kaikorai and take the juniors. Where are you going?' 'Back to the Priory,' I said year after year. But in January, 1964, there was a small folded piece of paper with my name on it in my stall. I stared at it with disbelief. Then I opened it. *Sister Mary Stephen. 1964. St Catherine's, Invercargill.*

# Chapter 16

# The Deep South

I was shattered. I really believed I was like Gibraltar, immovable. St Dominic's was *my* place. If I'd had any sense I would have realised I had been kept there because I wasn't considered settled enough to be moved. Many of my group had told me openly it would be much better if I did get moved to another convent. They worried about my obvious attachment to the Priory. 'Steve's been at St Dominic's since she was a boarder. That's over thirteen years. It's not good for anyone to be stuck in one place so long.'

One of the most important things about moving was that it taught us we were not indispensible to any job. 'The cemeteries of the world are full of indispensible people' was a saying we really believed. I could be Mistress of Schools for five years in one convent and then be moved to become an assistant teacher in another. When we were directed to move to another job it was our strict duty to pass on all the details of our previous position. We were in real trouble if we didn't. In this way there were few hiccups in personnel movements and the old order remained fast.

I wanted to remain fast at St Dominic's. Now I was going back there from Teschemakers only to collect my packed cases (it was a rule that everyone packed at the end of every year in preparation for removal) and move south. 'You'll love Invercargill. The people are marvellous, friendly and warm.' I knew all this but I was grim and silent as I watched from the train the soft hills of Dunedin merge into the neat, chequered paddocks of Southland. The Sisters I was with were all very happy to be returning to the south, especially Sister Cecily going to North Invercargill. I knew I would see her often as the Sisters from Kew, Heidelberg and Bluff came into St Catherine's for feast days or Sunday retreats. St Catherine's was named after the great, sometimes controversial, fourteenth century Dominican Tertiary, Catherine of Siena, who supported the 'correct' Pope at the time when three were elected by different factions. She was an amazing mixture of politician and mystic, social worker and recluse, and her huge portrait hung in most Dominican convents.

This convent was built right beside the Basilica facing the main railway track. I did not find either building an architectural gem compared to the Gothic charm of St Joseph's Cathedral and the grandeur of St Dominic's. All night we heard the trains passing and crossing bells ringing, and it was a standing joke for the old hands to talk about the new community Sisters leaping out of bed at the first sound of the bell as we had been instructed, only to find it was for the 1am goods train. We arrived about noon and were very enthusiastically welcomed by the Sisters there. We had lunch and came out on to the verandah to wave at the Sisters going off to St Dominic's on the north-bound railcar. I burst into tears. Mother Raymond, my new Prioress, came over to me quickly. 'Grow up, Sister Stephen. We don't want any babies here.' She was right of course. I turned indoors, shamefaced, pulled myself together and got on with unpacking.

There were about thirty Sisters living at St Catherine's. Most of us taught at the secondary school or at the parish primary school, St Joseph's, next door. The whole Catholic block was on Tyne St in what seemed to be the industrial part of Invercargill. It was unbearably flat and ugly. I longed for the hills and harbour of Dunedin. But I was now plunged into the activity of preparing classes in both senior English and History and even Latin to form five. My Mistress of Schools was Sister Marie Therese, a woman of total devotion to teaching; efficient, meticulous and absolutely straight. She had taught me at school and gone to St Dominic's herself with my mother. She could sometimes annoy me with her demand for perfection. I remember her correcting my work book week after week for putting an unnecessary 'r' in the author of the textbook always referred to as Ma(r)mour. She set the same high standards for herself and commanded respect in all she did. I became what amounted to her secretary in the school system and learned a great deal of administrative detail, although I used to get exasperated at having to do everything in triplicate for her. She was not nicknamed Smuts for nothing.

The classes were big at St Catherine's but the girls were, as reported, responsive and lovely to teach, although not as university orientated as the pupils at St Dominic's. The commercial courses were the most popular with parents and girls who wanted steady jobs in the business community of Southland. The boarders stayed from Monday to Friday and returned home for weekends. One of the Sisters complained, 'We have to start each week with table manners'. We lived very close to them until the new wing was built in 1965. We slept in cells on the top floor and the boarders on the second. Many of the girls from St Catherine's went on to become nuns themselves in the 1940s, '50s and '60s and I could see why. There was a warm family relationship between Sisters and girls.

This was the first time I had come into contact with Maori pupils and I loved Susan Toromata and the others from Bluff – their dignity, their warmth and in particular, as I discovered coaching them for various speech contests, their instinctive flair for oratory. Susan was a talented pianist and she explained in great technical detail to me the musical genius of the Beatles. This was the year of the great tour and train loads of fans went up to Dunedin to go to their concert. We were swept along with the new craze too. 'They're lovely, clean-shaven young boys,' Mother Raymond pronounced definitively and part of our recreation was to watch them on television. They were very funny.

Mother Raymond would now be regarded as a feminist. She believed that we relied on men too much – girls could do anything. As young nuns we proved that point; she taught us how to make concrete paths, linking various parts of the sprawling convent to others. She gave us all garden plots to look after and we did as much of our own repair work as possible. We also took turns at getting up at 5am on Friday morning to do the entire laundry for the convent. It took place in the basement under the heating ducts and pipes and we splashed around moving enormous piles of wet laundry from brass coppers to concrete sinks through hand wringers that crashed apart with alarming regularity. Then we moved up to the chapel at six to contemplate the eternal truths.

At the beginning of my four years at St Catherine's the chapel was a converted classroom at the front of the building. Mother Raymond was Prioress when the new three-storeyed convent wing and splendid octagonal chapel were added to St Catherine's. 'No house can be too good for God,' she said, with true medieval philosophy. She also saw the potential of a former bacon factory adjoining the playing fields. Within a year of its purchase it was transformed into a modern gymnasium and home economics unit. She was a reserved, self-disciplined woman with vision. I respected her immensely but needed to feel that she liked me. I did have an abject desire to please those in authority and to be told I was doing a good job. Not many Superiors saw that as important. 'A nun should be above praise or blame' was often quoted. I should be working only for God, but He kept pretty quiet about how I was shaping. So did Mother Raymond.

We had a retreat that year from a reputedly saintly Dominican Father and he gave spiritual lectures on prayer and self-giving. In confession I told him of my doubts about what God expected of me. There was a long pause. Then he said, 'You have fallen very low, Sister. Pray that God will forgive your lack of generosity from the depths of His compassion and start building your spiritual life again.' He didn't tell me how and I don't know what I expected him to say, but I came out of that retreat feeling totally listless. Everyone else raved about how wonderful it had been. I said nothing. I felt more of an alien than ever.

About this time my brother Emmet delighted the family with the news that he wanted to join the Marist Order, his teachers at St Bede's. He was accepted into the novitiate at Greenmeadows. He came to say goodbye and I too felt proud of him. He was eighteen, good looking and a warm and funny person. Part of me wondered how he would cope, but to express any doubts was unthinkable. I could not be a spoiler. If I was having doubts I shouldn't spread my cynicism to my brother. I knew I wouldn't see him now for about six years while he did his training, but we wrote stiff, artificially encouraging letters to each other as if we were superficial friends rather than brother and sister. We had done what all Catholic families were exhorted to — two of the four children had given themselves to God.

I put on a great show of happiness whenever my parents came to visit. I could not tell them how I really felt because it would have been a great and numbing disappointment, to my mother especially. Or so it seemed. Being a nun meant that I had closed off areas of emotional intimacy with my family and I felt that if I started to talk openly I would go to pieces — and what could they do? To leave now, after making final vows would have involved making a formal application for dispensation to Mother Prioress General and the councillors (the rules cited physical or mental illness as sufficient reason). If they accepted one's case it was then sent on by them to the

Congregation of Religious in Rome. It could take months of arguing and examination before a dispensation from solemn vows would come through. I knew of no one who had done it cleanly; it always seemed a very messy business and was never discussed openly in community. Nevertheless I felt more determined after that retreat to leave. It would be easier, I thought, if I wrote a formal letter to Mother David rather than see her personally again. I said that I wanted to apply for a dispensation from vows because for over ten years, as she knew, I had felt out-of-place, unsettled and unhappy.

Soon after, Mother David arrived in Invercargill and I was put through the same old rigmarole – 'You have bouts of uncertainty and unhappiness Sister. We all do. It will pass. Ask God, who loves you dearly for the strength you need.' It was even harder this time to believe in the promised sense of stability and fulfilment. I knew my resolve was weakening. At my Final Profession I had quite deliberately prayed – not for 'perseverance in religious life' as we were instructed – but simply for the grace to love God always. I was even on that most solemn day, deliberately leaving a door open.

So whenever my parents came in their new Ford Zephyr (my father had become the New Zealand correspondent for Time/Life magazines and there was more money), I showed them all over the convent and laughed and talked about many cabbages and kings but never about what I really felt. I was getting older, twenty-seven, twenty-eight; where was I really going? I felt bleak and a fraud being part of a vibrant community and yet more and more alienated from it. Then we had a change of Prioress.

# Chapter 17

# The Day of Reckoning

PERSONALITY conflicts do not seem to be part of a nun's life in the public's conception, but they do happen. In our day they were to be suppressed, like so much else. When Mother Gertrude was appointed Prioress at St Catherine's I had grave misgivings. She had taught me when I was a schoolgirl at St Dominic's and I had been terrified of her. I could never be at ease with her. How would it be now? At first we both tried hard. I was given new responsibilities on the theory perhaps that I would be too busy to be moodily introspective. With no training at all in accountancy and absolutely no head for figures, I was appointed Procuratrix in charge of the monies and the general mechanical running order of the convent – a sort of works manager. I was worried out of my mind. My office was in my cell, and from there I sent out accounts to all the pupils, paid cheques, issued receipts and at the same time I was teaching secondary classes, and music.

The one joy of my life was the junior choir. I was given charge of them, something I had never experienced before and

I relished it. We were deputed to sing at various services in the Basilica, and I thought they were beautiful singers. Mother Gertrude agreed and congratulated me. I was thrilled because I knew her standards of perfection in choral singing. But the old cynicism was still there; the unwise questioning of accepted attitudes. This was the time of Vatican II and the enormous upheaval in Catholic thinking that it caused. I thought Pope John XXIII was a darling, but it would take a long time for his liberalism to filter through. I remember Mother taking us young Sisters for a spiritual talk on some Vatican II documents. She began, 'We have always believed that the religious life was the highest calling of all in the Church. Now we are asked to believe,' and there was distinct incredulity in her voice, 'that all walks of life can glorify God equally well.'

This was the beginning of the end for me. I could see all sorts of possibilities that had never been countenanced before. Surely one could serve God just as well out in that world we had renounced? There had always been saints who had been married. Weren't we nuns becoming an anachronism? Were we reaching the people we were meant to be reaching? The old certainties were beginning to crumble and I secretly rejoiced. I once spoke to Sister Cecily, my old boarding school friend. 'Steve, be careful,' she said, 'you're becoming cynical.' I worried that I could disaffect others so I kept quiet. But I knew she was right.

About this time the film *The Sound of Music* came out and an Invercargill theatre kindly offered to show all the Sisters the film for free one Sunday afternoon. What a magnificent romance! However, Maria did not want to leave the convent and I did, and there weren't many widowed army majors living in baronial splendour around Dunedin or Invercargill. During this year my very dear old friend, Monsignor Hussey, collapsed and died. I felt keenly the loss of someone so sane and approachable. And my former pupil, Sandra, decided to enter the Order, and after staying with my family came to Invercargill to see me. I was in a quiet turmoil. Here she was, full of enthusiasm to enter the Order and I was considering leaving. I could never question her choice. Rather, I felt relieved that I had never put her off from the concept of religious life, consciously or unconsciously, while I was her teacher. Sandra would be a splendid nun. I wanted to tell her that as I said goodbye, but Mother Gertrude said I should not see myself as Sandra's particular mentor or take any credit for her entering. She may have been right, but what she said hurt. I was permitted only a three-minute meeting with Sandra before she left for the novitiate, and felt both tense and hyprocritical.

Whatever I did I could not please Mother Gertrude. I believe now that she knew I did not want to be a nun and unconsciously she was the catalyst to my finally leaving. I failed to meet so many of the standards she set. I had to rewrite all the cheques I had given her to sign as my Procuratrix signature was 'too untidy to be sent from an educational institution'. I was too noisy at recreation, too worldly in my conversation; all true I fear, and cumulatively I felt I was not making any grade at all. She informed Mother David that I was unsettled, when I thought I was improving. In the middle of all this my brother left the Marist seminary where he had been training now for four years and returned to Christchurch. Some of my friends wondered aloud whether I was affected by this. I was. I was almost excited. If my mother felt keen disappointment she did not show it. Emmet had tried for four years and had decided it was not for him. He had been helped in his decision by his spiritual directors and he seemed to leave with no sour feelings on either side. I secretly envied his clean break. When he came down to see me he had started university at Canterbury, had met Aileen, his future wife, and looked settled and adjusted. If he could do it, why couldn't I? Did I have to go through the whole old argument again of accepting what God was supposed to be wanting for me, the reluctant capitulation, the beautiful ideal that never seemed to match reality? I had reached the end of listening and talking. I had to act by myself. I had to break the habit of dependence.

In May 1967 we had our usual three-day retreat. It was meant to be a recharging of spiritual batteries, but I only went through the motions of listening. I felt dead. Nothing moved my feelings or conscience any more. At the same time the boiler furnace in the basement broke down and each day I had to break retreat to call in the plumber but he couldn't seem to get it right. I was getting irate notes from Mother Gertrude. Would I please ensure that the furnace was running correctly. The Sisters couldn't sleep at night for the sound of running water. I pursued the plumber by phone and he got annoyed. He was doing all he could. He was trying different techniques and it needed time to work. Couldn't I be a little patient?

We were due to come out of retreat on Sunday morning, Pentecost Sunday and Mother's Day. I was refectorian (in charge of the dining room), bellringer for the week and had grounds duty, checking on the security of all outside doors and gates. On Saturday I decided to phone home and ask my mother to come and get me. I did not even consider her reaction. I acted with the instinct of a child desperately looking to its mother for help. On Sunday we were to have a special post-retreat feast, and a mystery thriller film, *Woman of Straw* had been ordered for the evening's entertainment. It seemed totally appropriate.

I carefully arranged for others to do my duties – this would be in order if a Sister had been given permission to sleep in for any reason. I hoped they would presume that I had been given such permission. I rang home when I had finished serving lunch, while the community was eating. It was of course a collect call and my mother was cheerful and surprised. She had forgotten I was in retreat and thought I was ringing early for Mothers' Day. I was tense and jumpy. I wanted to leave. I didn't want to speak to anyone – not to Mother David, a priest – no one. I just wanted out immediately. Could she come and pick me up about 9pm from the back gate? I think now I was in total shock. How, in my senses, could I have expected anyone to drive from Christchurch to Invercargill on a winter's day, leaving at 1.30pm? What a demand!

My mother was absolutely marvellous. She was very calm and said that my letters had seemed forced and unnatural lately, and the family had thought something was wrong. She would be there as soon after nine as possible and, no, if I thought it was unwise, she would not contact Mother David or anyone else. I hung up and went back to refectory duties, my head buzzing. I felt like Macbeth planning Duncan's murder with his wife – I had 'settled and bent up / each corporal agent to this terrible feat'. Because it was a retreat, the junior Sisters had left their cells to the visitors and were in cubicles in the boarders' new dormitory. I carefully packed a case there with underclothes and a few of my own treasured books and pushed it under the bed.

I may have seemed calm but one or two stark questions monopolised my thinking. How could I leave students who were facing important examinations? I answered that to myself by arguing I would be in no fit state to teach anyone soon if I stayed. I knew that I was committing a heinous crime but I also knew that it was heinous only in convent circles or Catholic minds. I believed in God and hoped that in spite of all this He would still love me. I no longer felt anything about letting Him down. I had been told so often, 'You will never be happy if you leave. You will feel cheated all your life'. I remember saying quite fiercely to myself, 'I don't care. I can never be as unhappy as I am now'. In the end I blotted out all thinking.

Somehow I served tea, went to Office, kept up the charade of listening to the final retreat sermon. At ten to nine most of the community were on their way to bed. I locked up all the doors except the one I was going to leave from. I rang the nine o'clock Profound Silence bell, went to my cubicle, took off my habit and folded it into the cupboard. I moved the pillow into the bed to look as if I was there and pulled the side curtains. I wondered about my Profession ring with its lovely Pauline motto, 'to me, to live is Christ. To die is a great gain'. My parents had given it to me when I made Solemn Profession. I took it off my ring finger, feeling I was no longer worthy to wear it and placed it on the wardrobe shelf. In my dressing gown, slippers and night veil I padded quietly down to the far gate. It was ten past nine.

# CHAPTER 18

# DEBRIEFING

THE back street was as usual very quiet at nine on a Saturday night. It was a cold, crisp night and from inside the gate I could hear any vehicle that moved outside. None did. About nine-twenty it began to snow. I was very cold but I didn't notice because a terrible fear had gripped me – there had been an accident – my mother had been killed, and it was undoubtedly my fault. I went numb inside as the awful realisation came home to me. Not only that, but I would have to go back inside, face the future and start all over again. I felt paralysed in that corner between the hall door and the brick wall, and I began to cry. Suddenly, at nine-thirty, I heard a car pull up. I waited till I heard a voice and then I rushed to the gate and pulled it open. My mother and sister Marian fell out of both front doors, took one look at me in the street light and burst out laughing. That truly saved my sanity. I had never appreciated being laughed at so much before. I realised how ridiculous I must have looked standing there in my dressing gown with my night veil awry, at nine-thirty at night.

The relief was so intense that I began shivering and crying all at once and they took off my night veil, put a woollen beret on my head and bundled me into the back seat. We sped away out of Invercargill in the snow. I have no recollection of the car trip except that I wanted to get clear of Southland and Otago. There were no Dominican convents in Christchurch and I felt safe only when we had passed Oamaru. It was appallingly selfish of me to want to carry on – my mother and Marian must have been exhausted but they kept on driving. I fell asleep in the back and they kept themselves going with flasks of coffee. I was later told of how the car ran out of petrol in Milton. My mother discovered she had not enough money and had to borrow from the highly suspicious priest at the Milton presbytery – but I had no inkling of it. All I can feel looking back on those two days is an immense – quite immense – sense of gratitude from child to mother that I can never repay no matter how many other Mother's Days there are.

We reached Christchurch at about 6.30am and I do remember vividly my father's face as he saw me coming up the drive. It was an expression of disbelief, then delight. I knew I was at home.

My first reaction was physical. I hated the tiny cramped box that was our home. I hated its low ceilings. I think that feeling lasted for fifteen minutes. My mother gave me a very strong hot toddy and I was put into my sister's bed while the family held an excited conference in the living room. I slept as I had never slept before.

At 10am Mother Gertrude rang from Invercargill. 'Do you know where your daughter is?' was her terse question.

My mother answered calmly, 'Which one?' The exchange was not friendly and next Mother David rang. She had been in the North Island when she was given the news and was flying back to Dunedin. Could I meet her at the Christchurch airport? My mother said firmly no, I was sleeping. Then at four in the afternoon a call came from the Christchurch Catholic cathedral presbytery – Bishop Ashby wished to visit us. Now Bishop Ashby was a family friend. As children we had played at his house with his brothers and sisters and loved his Aunt Kate – we all called her Aunt Cake because she was the kind of aunt who loved all children and gave us the most delicious biscuits and cakes when we visited. Bishop Ashby was in a very embarrassing situation. I had broken a rule of the congregation and a Canon Law pertaining to professed nuns. I had run away. I was out of Bishop Kavanagh's diocese and in his, and Bishop Kavanagh had told him to deal with me.

He wanted to see me alone but my father insisted on being present because he knew what I had meant by moral bullying. He knew that I had buckled so often before to well-meaning but authoritarian tactics. 'You won't be happy.' 'Have you thought about this serious step properly?' 'Are you doing what God wants or what Judith wants?' 'We all have our down moments.' 'You are just going through a phase.' I had heard them all before and my father needn't have worried. I was grateful for his presence but I was not in a mood to quail before any representative of authority. Bishop Ashby was equally firm. My mother too must have felt suddenly guilty at aiding and abetting my escape. When she opened the door to the Bishop, she said, 'I am beginning to realise the enormity of what I have done.' 'Enormity,' he snorted, 'is not the word!' I had broken a law of the Church and I was therefore excommunicated. I could not receive the sacraments of the Church. I was no longer considered a member.

To my own surprise I received the news with detachment. I held on to the fact that I loved God, a God who was good, and all this was something else. Theologians might call this selective morality, but I selected to live a life where I could love God by being what He had made me, not trying to be somebody else. My youngest sister Marian was far more shattered than I was at this exposure to the legalism of the Church. She made a commitment to Quakerism several years later for a variety of reasons, one of them being a rejection of a legalistic church. Bishop Ashby then pointed out that if I wanted to leave legally from a convent I needed to be in a convent. Would I return to the Dominicans? I was utterly but quietly adamant that I would not go to one of the Dominican convents and face the pressure to stay that I had faced on so many earlier occasions. Would I go to a convent of another Order for a short period of time, like three weeks? I could legally apply to Rome for dispensation of vows from that convent. He suggested the Cenacle Sisters of Wellington, an American Order who had recently moved to New Zealand. I agreed, because deep down I wanted to do things correctly. I wanted to be formally dispensed from my vows. I was therefore to fly to Wellington and the Convent of the Cenacle in Woburn as soon as possible.

I realised what a financial strain this was placing on my parents. I had taken the customary dowry of a hundred pounds when I entered the Order and I had signed it over to them when I made a will before Final Profession. I left, of course, with no money at all and no secular clothes. My parents had had to drive all the way to Invercargill and back to get me and now they had to pay for my airfare to Wellington. And more than that, I couldn't fly there in a dressing gown and beret, so I had to be outfitted. Shopping for those first clothes wasn't an exciting experience. I just had to look relatively normal.

Those first days at home were very confusing. Even small things like talking and eating at the same time made me uneasy. My sister Gill gave me some of her *Vogue* magazines to read and I was appalled at their glossiness and superficiality. Suddenly I was aware of what worldliness was – where were my spiritual props, my half-hour's meditation, the Divine Office? I told myself that spirituality did not depend on location. God was a spirit and I did not have to be in a special place to find Him. No matter how uneasy the transition was I was never going back.

A day or so later I flew to Wellington. We had a wonderful priest friend who had taught Emmet at St Bede's called Father Bernie Ryan S.M. He was then in Wellington and my parents arranged for him to pick me up at the airport. He always has been a very special person – never more so than when I met him again that day. I was feeling very down when I left home. I knew I would be back, but when? And I also felt the awful cut-off of excommunication; for a Catholic, it is the most serious punishment of all – officially you are no longer a member of the Church. I could go to mass but not receive communion, and if I died I would not be in a state of grace. I didn't feel I had done anything to be cut off from God but if I had I was truly sorry. Father Ryan heard my confession and told me I could receive communion. Of all the officials I dealt with in the Church at that time, he represented the human face; his kindness was real and humble. 'If God doesn't love you,' he said, 'what's to become of buggers like me?' I could see why he later became Superior General of his Order in Rome.

Father Bernie's parents lived in Lower Hutt, and when he took me to the Cenacle Convent he arranged with the Mother Superior for me to be allowed to visit his parents, Joe and Mary. They were a wonderful couple in their late seventies and Mary took me under her wing. In those three weeks in Lower Hutt she took me to downtown Wellington, to the fashion department in Kirkcaldie and Stains, encouraging me to try on some outfits. In her quiet, no-nonsense way she was getting me used to the way of the world again. She and Joe would take me to weekday mass at St Mary's, Boulcott Street. They accepted me simply as I was, which was even more amazing as three of their four children had become priests or nuns.

The Sisters of the Cenacle were also warm and welcoming. I was given a small, comfortable room and asked if I could help in their library and do their shopping. This took some courage at first as I felt everyone in the shops was looking at me with my ridiculously short hair and general timidity. After all, I hadn't been in a shop for twelve years. The Mother Superior, Mother Ryan coincidentally, was a young New Zealander, a positive woman who made me feel quite normal and never once preached to me. I discovered that Mother David had told them I was in too emotional a state to make a serious decision like leaving the Order and that I was to be psychologically assessed by the Cenacle Sisters before I wrote my formal letter to Rome. Hence the three weeks. Mother Ryan told me later that in the first fifteen minutes of our meeting she knew I had left religious life for good and that I was neither emotionally disturbed nor mentally unstable. I was allowed to go to mass with the community but other than that I worked on my own in the library. It was a period of calm self-assessment and I had no backward thoughts at all.

I received letters regularly. One pile came from Dunedin where many of the Sisters with whom I had been in the novitiate wrote asking me to return. I knew they had been told to write and I felt sad, like Hamlet with Rosencrantz and Guildenstern. My father must have realised this would happen and every day there was a letter from him – short, inconsequential and funny. He told me later he wanted to make sure I would not be influenced to return by any emotional manipulation. I loved him for doing such a chore but he needn't have worried. I was quietly immune from any such emotive tugs on my early loyalties.

# CHAPTER 19

# 'GEORGIE GIRL'

WHEN the three weeks were up Mother Ryan reported to Mother David that I was ready to leave the Order and that I was capable of making such a decision. Mother David replied that I was to live an 'exclaustrated life', living under the three vows, poverty, chastity and obedience, at my parents' home until my dispensation came through from Rome. That could take about six to eight weeks. I carefully wrote my formal application for dispensation. I had known of other Sisters who had left in recent years and they had gone with reasons like 'mental illness', 'nervous breakdown', 'physically unfit for the rigours of the religious life'. I knew that none of these reasons could be mine and I wanted one that answered finally what I had always been told, 'God loves you especially; he is asking more of you than of the others'. I wrote simply, 'I request the permission of the Congregation of Religious Orders to be dispensed from my vows of Profession as I no longer have the generosity to follow religious life in the Dominican Order.' No one could argue against that.

I left the Cenacle nuns with real gratitude to Mother Ryan for all she and the Sisters had done for me, and flew back to Christchurch. I was extremely happy and longed to be home, low ceilings, small rooms and all. The whole family was at the airport to meet me and we had a very happy and laughing meal together that night. On the plane I had been seated beside a businessman who talked to me about his job – he ran a night club at New Brighton. I realise now he thought I was fair game, asking me if he could take me there. I beamed at him seraphically, 'I don't know what I'll be doing. I'm just so happy to be going home. I wish I could share my happiness with you.' My family fell apart when I told them this and their whole aim from then on was to teach me to behave like a twenty-nine year old.

My father said I was to go to the movies – *My Fair Lady* and *Cat Ballou* would do me good; so would *What's New, Pussycat*. My sisters supervised my wardrobe and tried to make my very short hair more presentable. My mother bought me a pair of contact lenses so that I began to look less and less like Sister Stephen and more like Judith. I still ached for some sort of organised spirituality in my life. I missed the Office and meditation immensely, so went along with my sister, Gill, to a series of Catholic lectures given at the university at Ilam by a visiting theologian. An old friend of the family saw Gill and came over, looked at me hard and said, as I was busy looking away, 'It isn't Judith, is it?' She was very kind but I couldn't escape fast enough. I dreaded meeting Catholics; I was a runaway nun and that was not acceptable and I didn't want to talk about it or justify myself to anyone. A Catholic neighbour of ours, a well-educated married woman, asked me to tea. In the course of talking she suddenly said, 'Well, you know, it's all very well for you to walk out of your vows. We married people can't leave our husbands.' I was numb with guilt and could think of no answer.

It was the same when I wrote, foolishly, to my former spiritual director, Father T. P. Fitzgerald, then living in Australia. I thought I was being courteous in explaining what I had done. I said that my leaving would be a nine days' wonder in the convent but that the commotion would pass quickly. Three weeks later I received his reply in the mail and the stinging coldness of his tone and comments caused me to burst into tears. 'I hope, should you ever marry, you have more respect for your marriage vows than you have shown towards your religious ones.' I had underestimated his loyalty to the Order. My father who saw my distress, read the letter and put it on the fire. It was an important lesson in making a total break with the past.

It became clear very quickly to me that I had to find work. My parents were never well off, and I could see they were pouring money they could not easily spare into my rehabilitation. The injustice of this made me write to Mother David requesting some money to help, once my dispensation came through. I had worked, teaching for the Order for twelve years and, at the age of twenty-nine, I could no longer look to my parents for financial support. Nowadays any Sister who leaves gets a lump sum to help her set herself up. Then, I felt like a beggar. But after the dispensation came through my hundred pound dowry was returned to me.

Teaching was what I enjoyed and teaching was where I would find work. In May 1967, I did not know where to look. My parents knew a Miss Natalie Simpson in the secondary inspectorate of the Department of Education in Christchurch. I phoned her and she told me that there was an English and History job at Westport. She told me how to apply. But my father felt I was not ready to go flatting – he would not have stopped me but suggested I go in to the Department, see the inspectors who had visited me at St Catherine's several weeks earlier, identify myself and find out whether there was a job in Christchurch.

Gill had lent me her bright cherry coat which I thought was beautiful, but in reality was a hideous, traffic-stopping colour. I wore it when I went in to the inspectorate and met Mr Jack Haglund. He had seen me take a History class a month before when I was Sister Stephen at St Catherine's. I told him who I was and his reaction was amazing. He sprang out of his seat, shook my hand warmly and then took me along the corridor shouting to anyone in particular, 'Do you remember Sister Stephen? Here she is!' I was completely embarrassed at being such an unexpected celebrity. The guilt I felt made me want to remain faceless and anonymous. He took me into an end room to meet Miss Nan Anderson who had also just inspected me at St Catherine's and whose impeccable style of dressing had vastly impressed me.

While she and Mr Haglund tried to find a school in Christchurch which wanted an English/History teacher mid-year, I looked at the other occupant of the room. He was an elegantly tall man in his late thirties with beautifully fine hands and eyes that suggested past sorrows. I noticed the name on his desk – Reg Graham. He suggested Christ's College might be interested and he rang the then Headmaster, Mr Nigel Creese, who said he would prefer a male teacher. All the inspectors promised they would let me know of any vacancy, and I went home quite hopeful. Two phone calls followed. There was an immediate relieving job at Christchurch Girls' High School for a week – would I see the headmistress? Then Natalie Simpson rang to ask if I would try for the job advertised at Christchurch Boys' High School. Knowing what the Christ's College reaction had been, I was loath to do so but she insisted. I wrote out the application form and started the next week on the relieving job at Girls' High. It was a relief indeed to go back to the routine of teaching but I felt a total alien in the staffroom. Miss Robinson the headmistress was very kind, but I got the distinct feeling that there wasn't much difference between the hierarchical structure of the convent and the staffroom of this school.

A week or so later I was called to an interview with Mr Charles Caldwell in his impressive study at Christchurch Boys'. He was a man who wasted no words. He asked me a few questions about my teaching experience, made no reference at all to my convent past, and offered me the job. I accepted it with some excitement. My father was aghast. 'Are you sure you want to teach in an all-male establishment? You're tougher than I thought you were.' And so in term two of 1967 I began taking Mr Roy Palmer's classes at Christchurch Boys' High School while he had a year's leave in the States. It was one of my happiest teaching experiences.

Was it just that I enjoyed male company after twelve years in an all-female environment? Was it that I felt the entire staff regarded me as their younger sister? Indeed I loved the staff-room and its old identities – Wally Mapplebeck, Frank Allen, Colin Macintosh (who was to be my headmaster at Rangiora High School years later), Jim Chalmers, David Sinclair and so many others. They were all genuinely kind and I blossomed. The new song out then was 'Georgie Girl' and it became my theme song. 'Life is a reality; you can't always run away. Don't be so scared of changing and rearranging yourself. It's time for jumping down from the shelf.'

# Chapter 20

# Rearrangements

ABOUT four weeks after I had started at Christchurch Boys' High there was a message for me at home. Mother David had received the dispensation form from Rome and had come to Christchurch for the final signing. I was to meet her at Calvary Hospital. My brother Emmet and his wife Aileen had a flat in Bealey Avenue and he took time to drive me there and wait outside. My family's support in that year was something I will never forget. This was the hardest moment of all because Mother David had always been so kind to me. She had acted in what she believed were my best interests. It was she who had urged me to reconsider so many times before, making me feel I was a special favourite of God, and I had to steel myself to make this final and irrevocable severance. I felt I was knifing her in the back. She was very tense and her attempts at cheerfulness were brittle. She asked me once again whether I was sure that this was what I wanted and I said quietly and firmly, 'Yes'. She began to cry softly and I found my hand wobbling as I signed the document that laicised me once and for all. I was freed from the vows I had taken so long ago. She kissed me, we said goodbye and I walked quickly outside to Emmet.

I never saw her again until Mother Catherine Laboure, once my Prioress, let me know that Mother David was terminally ill at Teschemakers. I visited her before she died and we finally accepted each other's position and I apologised for the pain I knew I had caused her. I am glad I made the effort to see her. After I had signed my laicisation Bishop Ashby called me in to the cathedral presbytery. He was much kinder to me, almost relieved. I had to kneel and recite the psalm 'Miserere mei Domine' which I did. Then I was formally forgiven and received back into the Church. He asked me about my new teaching job and wished me luck.

Little by little some old school friends heard that I was home and they decided to get me into the social scene. Fleur was then married to Michael and living in the Hakataramea Valley and she organised a welcome home party. While the whole weekend was a lot of fun, I wasn't really interested in the dating game. I was twenty-nine, my hair was still appalling and I had decided to make teaching my life. Who, I reasoned, would want a twenty-nine year old virgin?

Part of me still deeply missed my friends in the convent. One weekend that winter I was invited to Dunedin to visit family friends. My father said quite firmly, 'Make no attempt to get in touch with anyone in the convent. You will only regret it.' But I couldn't resist ringing Sister John Baptist who had entered with me twelve years before. She was the only one of our six still in Dunedin, at Santa Sabina convent in North East Valley. No one recognised my voice when I rang and when she came to the phone she begged me to come and see her. 'I'm dying to see what you look like,' she said. 'Come up to the side door and I'll let you in.'

How stupid of me! We had a marvellous fifteen minutes talking non-stop, among other things, of the convent version of how I had left and the shock it had caused at St Catherine's. Suddenly the parlour door opened and the Mother Superior walked in. She totally ignored me and said, 'Sister, will you please return to your duties. You have no permission to see this visitor.' She held the door as Sister Baptist left, and did not look at me at all. I was left to find my own way out, like a dog with its tail between its legs, realising how right my father had been.

The only other contact I had was a much happier one. Mother Laboure, who always kept in touch, was passing through Christchurch and she rang me from Rosary House – would I come and see her? She was exactly as she always was with me; kind, accepting, non-judgmental. But she said something even kinder than usual. 'I think you had a temporary vocation, Judith. Some people are called to serve God as Religious, not for life but for a certain period, and I think that was your situation.' It was the first time I felt I wasn't a traitor and deserter in the eyes of the Church.

Meanwhile my hair was growing longer and I was becoming more confident about my appearance. I still relied on my sisters to tell me what colours to wear and there were some gross mistakes. I remember once a sixth form boy coming up after a class and asking me very politely and earnestly, 'Please, Miss Hobbs, please don't wear that dress again.' He was really quite distressed. I made verbal gaffs that were just as bad, telling the same sixth formers to bring their 'Sieman' (the author of a current History textbook) to class the next day, and they looked rather unnerved by the suggestion. And I caused an uproar in the fifth form by asking a noted rake to explain the proverb, 'a bird in the hand is worth two in the bush'. I hope he married an ardent feminist.

That year at Boys' High was memorable. Without exception the staff were kind and I enjoyed every day there. They taught me the important rubrics of rugby when I watched the Saturday school games. I also learnt how to drive a car, encouraged by the gentlemanly David Sinclair. Every Friday after school the staff went to Nancy's pub on Riccarton Road for a relaxed session, and they asked me if I would come too for an hour or so. My father thought it might be a good idea and I struggled through a mug of beer at many a session. It was the fact that they asked me to join them on what was a very male ritual, and looked after me and drove me home – provided I'd been the one to talk to the Salvation Army lady for them – that I appreciated.

In November of 1967, six months after I returned home, my father died suddenly. It had been a hot day and he had come from work visibly tired. After dinner he went out to the kitchen and there was an awful crash. We all rushed in and found him lying unconscious on the floor. He died minutes later, before the ambulance got there. He was fifty-four. Looking back, I am immensely grateful that I had had those six months with him. He was the wisest and kindest of men and I loved his Chaucerian humour. He had not achieved his great dream of producing the definitive New Zealand novel though he had written three moderately successful books. The first one was the one I loved the best, *The Wild West Coast* and that had been published while I was at St Dominic's. He had given me a copy – 'To my firstborn, the first copy of my first book'. Foolishly, years later, I lent it to someone and never saw it again. He may not have been the most responsible of fathers but his humanity and values were his greatest bequest to us.

# CHAPTER 21

# 'SOME ENCHANTED EVENING'

I taught at Boys' High from May 1967 till August 1968. About July of 1968 we were visited by inspectors. In the convent this visit always struck fear in the school that we would somehow be found wanting, but the Boys' High staff were very blasé. On the arrival of the inspectors, Mike Lindroos, a Geography teacher, came flying into the staffroom and greeted me with, 'We've found the man for you. He's an inspector; he taught me in Dunedin and I like him. He's single and he's wealthy'. I professed a mild interest in such a happy combination of qualities. The staff had been sorting out several likely candidates for me for quite some time. Their brotherly efforts to see me happily settled were often hilarious, if fruitless, endeavours. The man in question was pointed out – Reg Graham, about whom I had speculated on my first visit to the Department. I was now to meet him as my inspector.

The whole idea of an inspection was that the hapless teacher would be visited unexpectedly, and presumably off-guard. One never knew when the inspector would walk in, go to the back of the room, watch, listen, take notes and occasionally look at always the untidiest exercise books of the untidiest boys. This inspector told me exactly when he would come, halfway through my English class with the fifths. It was a Wednesday afternoon, the period just before the school was dismissed for rugby. We had been studying Keats' poetry and I felt the 'Ode on a Grecian Urn' could produce no untoward surprises. Mr Graham came in and moved to the back. The front row of quiet, normally well-behaved youths suddenly developed facial tics which the inspector could not see. Then Hanafin put up his hand and asked me to explain the meaning of 'unravish'd' in the first line. I hope I handled the question coolly, but the experience was unnerving and I felt that the attractive Mr Graham would be appalled at my ineptitude. He made a few positive comments and disappeared, but I was suddenly smitten. I blamed Keats.

For weeks afterwards I wondered whether I would ever see him again. Mike Lindroos gave me all the personal details ('he likes *West Side Story*, he writes poetry, he loves fast cars') and it became the English staff's mission to have us meet again. I attended every English seminar Mr Graham spoke at, but he never seemed to notice me. In August, St Bede's Old Boys held a ball at the Winter Gardens and my brother Emmet and his wife Aileen were going with a large group. Would I like to come? He could 'jack up' a partner for me. I did not like the idea of a blind date at all. The only person I wanted to go with was Reg Graham, but how?

In the staffroom among all the old identities was Mr Gordon Troup, a much-loved French teacher. He was obviously a man of the world and I asked him discreetly whether I should ring and ask Mr Graham to partner me to this, my first ball. He looked at me earnestly and said at length, 'Most women wouldn't get away with it but I think you just might'. I enlisted the aid of Marian, my youngest sister. She found Mr Graham's phone number and told me I was to screw my courage to its sticking place and ring him in the interval between the news and the weather sections on television. We said not a word to my mother. She would have been appalled at such forward behaviour. I rang. He answered. I could hear music playing in the background and panicked – he was probably entertaining. I stuttered out my name and he asked me to speak up, he couldn't hear. With enormous audacity, I reminded him of his inspection visit and, realising I could be downgraded immediately by the Department if this went wrong, asked if he would partner me to St Bede's ball. He said he'd be delighted to and made a note of the time and place. I put down the phone with a whoop of joy. My mother was disgusted but when Reg rang three days later to ask me to dinner first at the Russley, she decided he must be a gentleman to retake the initiative.

A black ball dress was chosen, jewellery and long white gloves. I felt like a sixteen year old and I was twenty-nine. I had never gone out socially by myself with a man before. My sisters decided I needed to know what drinks to order when asked. I had to appear sophisticated. There were the three 'D's; Dubonnet, Drambuie and I can't now remember the third, even though I rehearsed these names carefully at the time. At 7.30pm a car drove up; it was an elegant Citröen with height adjustment so that the car went down as you got in. Reg rang the front door bell. We owned two precious Burmese cats who panicked in front of strangers, so my mother opened the door a narrow slit to stop them bolting out. One looked keen to do just that, so Reg had the door inexplicably closed in his face. Eventually he was led into the sitting room and faced a row of female Hobbses. He was completely unnerved – we all talked fast, nervously and at cross purposes but he made a gallant effort to do justice to each of us, his head moving like a spectator at a tennis match. At the hotel I was thrown when he asked if I would like some hock. That wasn't in my list but I couldn't show my ignorance so dry old hock it was. I kept dropping my table napkin and pieces of cutlery but we did make it to the ball and we did have a wonderful night, coming home at 4.30am. My sister Gill had to come out to the kitchen for a glass of water as we were kissing goodbye and I remember reassuring her later that all was indeed well.

One long week went by and I heard nothing. He had gone skiing to Coronet Peak and by the end of that week I was telling myself it was better to have loved and lost. Then a postcard arrived, followed by several letters. Reg came back to Christchurch and after three weeks of going out together every day we became engaged. I was thirty and Reg was thirty-seven; well, what was the point of waiting?

My time at Boys' High was over – Mr Palmer was back. Mr Caldwell said he could give me a job in 1969 but he had no position available for term three of 1968. Would I be interested in a term's relieving job that was advertised at Nelson College? He'd ring the headmaster and recommend me. Reg wanted me to stay in Christchurch. Couldn't I take a job at a local school? But I felt I needed space to find out exactly how I regarded him. Also I had never lived entirely by myself before and this would be a chance to prove something to myself. I got the job and my mother remembered a flat she had heard of that was sometimes available in Collingwood Street right at the base of the Grampians. Mr and Mrs Nelson (!) welcomed me warmly and I rented their very pleasant ground floor flat for a term.

Mr Caldwell had very close friends there who, he said, would look after me – an English ex-RAF pilot and his Swedish wife. Robin and Brita Mordant became absolutely wonderful friends. Robin was a cricket fiend and after I had talked about Reg he asked me whether he played cricket. I had no idea. Robin was appalled. 'Ring him immediately and find out. Then I'll know whether he is a gentleman.' Sadly, Reg failed the test. There would be a phone call from Reg at least twice a week. On one memorable occasion I had been drinking some of Nelson's apple cider and the conversation on that toll call was more than usually one-sided. I was fairly bubbling.

When Robin and Brita invited Reg to stay with them on weekends, I would go into paroxysms of anxiety, preparing splendid meals in the flat. I had learnt how to make stew for forty last for two meals; now I was cooking for two people and this man was a superb cook. I would rush down to Mrs Nelson whenever the white sauce went lumpy – but I'm told I've never made a lemon chiffon pie as splendid as the one I made in Nelson. My cooking is not good – it's what Katherine Whitehorn refers to as 'basic slag'. I have a great tendency to leave something cooking while I rush off to do something else, so that when Reg is away he sometimes rings about teatime and begins by saying, 'I can smell it burning from here' – and it isn't passion.

We climbed the Grampians, heard the skylarks and behaved as all engaged couples behave. I was deliriously in love and it seemed that spring, 1968, was all it should have been in the best Cartland romances. Teaching at Nelson College was rather like being a visitor in a gentlemen's private club. The staff were painstakingly courteous but I was the only woman in their staffroom and it did put an understandable constraint on their behaviour. Basil Wakelin, the headmaster, seemed very stern in a military way but I discovered he had a wicked sense of humour. He once strode purposefully into my class, mid-lesson, glared at the students, and, with a conspiratorial wink, whispered, 'Miss Hobbs, God is watching you'. I felt He was indeed; I was deeply happy. I left Nelson in early December when Reg and I drove back to Christchurch to prepare for our wedding.

We were married in my parish church of St Joseph's, Papanui, on 20 December, 1968. It was a cloudless hot day. My brother Emmet gave me away and my two sisters were bridesmaids. And since then? The tapestry of a normal married life; two children born within a year of each other, Kirsty and Piers, one dark-haired, the other red, and both fiercely independent spirits.

The adjustment to secular life was not as easy as some observers might have thought. Reg and I, coming from such totally different backgrounds (he is not a Catholic), had probably more to give and take in our relationship than most married couples. But we have both grown and not, I feel, at each other's expense.

I returned to teaching, first part-time at Villa Maria, then eventually full time at Rangiora High School. In the middle of Reg's male menopause we moved to Singapore to teach at the Institute of Education for two years. We returned with relief to the temperate climate and the freedom and space of New Zealand. We had fourteen settled family years at Cust in North Canterbury, a period we all look back on with affection.

Now the wheel has come nearly full circle and we are back in Dunedin, excited at the prospect of a stimulating semi-retirement in our favourite city of hills and sea.

*Piers.*

*Kirsty with baby Will.*

*Reg and Judith. Family photographs taken 2006.*

# Epilogue

WHEN I started this exercise I was doing it for our children by way of explanation. But I was also aware of other motives – a need to put my side of the story, a desire to recall a way of life that is now gone.

There are still Dominican Sisters in convents in New Zealand, but these convents are no longer huge institutions. St Dominic's Priory is mostly empty, its cells and dormitories, its cloisters and reception rooms now large vacant spaces. Sometimes it serves as a temporary home for immigrants and the needy. The chapel has been restored and weekly mass is said there for the parishioners. I visited that Priory in 1987 to lay a few ghosts. I met them round every corner – the rattle of the rosary beads, the swirl of the white habit, the noise of pots and pans in the kitchen, the whispered conversations. I realised forcibly that buildings are really for people and I was sad to see the Priory as a rather tatty, neglected museum. I looked over the city from the weed-blown convent garden and felt even more strongly the freedom of spirit I now enjoy, a freedom I will never take for granted.

The Sisters do a great deal of social and parish work as

counsellors, funeral parlour assistants, accountants in diocesan offices. A few of them still teach. They live in groups of four and five in ordinary houses. The old hierarchies and structures of convent life, the penances, the rules, the order of the day, are gone for ever. Even wearing the white habit is optional. The Sisters I meet occasionally are very much individuals, responsible for their own lives. Or so it seems. In 1971 the Order celebrated a hundred years in New Zealand and a history was published. I searched in it for my name, for some record of those twelve years when I was a member of an illustrious community. Of course, it was not there. Possible embarrassment to either of us was thereby avoided, but I admit I felt cheated.

Yet I look back on those twelve years not bitterly, but with a quiet gratitude for the experience. I met people there I will always love and respect. I tried to live a way of life that was beautiful in its idealism but that demanded more in reality than I was prepared to give. I learnt a great deal about myself and perhaps too little of God.

I once heard a neighbour say of her dying mother, 'towards the end she was very anxious, tossing and turning in her bed not because she was in pain but because she could not find her God'.

And that has led me to think that when I come to die the God I hope to find will be the God Hamlet spoke of, 'There's a divinity that shapes our ends / rough-hew them how we will'.